Praise for *I Am Here: Postcards from My Daughter in Spirit*

"In her debut memoir, Togher presents wrenching and honest meditations on how to live after the passing of someone you love...Togher writes of her experience with courage and deep emotional intelligence. Her memoir reads as a therapeutic expression of her grief, a practical guide for readers seeking comfort after loss, and a celebration of Suzanne's (daughter) life."

—Publishers Weekly/BookLife

"Judith Jones Togher shares her deep love for her daughter in *I Am Here: Postcards from My Daughter in Spirit.*" I Am Here is therefore a highly spiritual story. The messages received by Judith Togher from Suzanne in Spirit are deep and profound and full of love.

—Tommy Wong, Readers' Favorite

"Through her experiences, readers receive keys on how to find, recognize, and use their own 'postcards' to develop a revised worldview and connections to spirit and deceased loved ones... [*I Am Here*] should be included on the reading lists of those recovering from grief."

—Midwest Book Review

I Am Here

*Postcards from
My Daughter in Spirit*

I Am Here

Postcards from
My Daughter in Spirit

Judith Jones Togher

IZZARD INK
PUBLISHING

IZZARD INK PUBLISHING

PO Box 522251

Salt Lake City, Utah 84152

www.izzardink.com

Library of Congress Cataloging-in-Publication Data

Names: Jones Togher, Judith, author.
Title: I am here : postcards from my daughter in spirit / Judith Jones Togher.
Description: First edition. | Salt Lake City, Utah : Izzard Ink Publishing, [2021]
Identifiers: LCCN 2021001288 | ISBN 9781642280630 (paperback) |
ISBN 9781642280623 (epub)
Subjects: LCSH: Death—Miscellanea. | Grief—Miscellanea. | Spiritualism. |
Parapsychology.
Classification: LCC BF1275.D2 J66 2021 | DDC 133.9—dc23
LC record available at https://lccn.loc.gov/2021001288

Cover Design by Susan Olinsky
Book Design by Alissa Theodor
Cover Images by shutterstock/Svetlana Micic

First Edition

Contact the author at info@izzardink.com
Paperback ISBN: 978-1-64228-063-0
eBook ISBN: 978-1-64228-062-3

Table of Contents

This book is dedicated to
my daughter Suzanne,
and to my husband Michael

Foreword

I lost a child. My youngest daughter died and I was so overcome with the darkness of grief that I wanted to die too. It was only when I knew she really was not far from me, and we could still communicate in a different way, that the darkness lifted and I began to heal and live the life I needed to live, in peace and in wonderment. I hope to convey ways for you to learn to recognize messages that your loved one may give you in Spirit, and to discover some techniques to help you through grief and loss toward healing and joy in life.

I don't believe in coincidence, but all things occur for a reason. From the people you bump into, to the kind word said by a stranger just when a kind word is needed, to finding a talisman like a found penny, or unexplained phenomena, Spirit speaks in lots of ways. Our loved ones make contact in different forms, if we watch and listen.

They use these forms because they know that in so doing, we will understand that they are reaching out to us from the other side. These messages I call "postcards" because they are small but significant and joyous contacts from Spirit.

Suzanne continues to leave us many postcard messages of one sort or another. For Mike and me, physical phenomena, sights, odors, movement of objects, and the playful use of lights and sounds show us she is near. As you will read, the amazing appearance of pennies as our special talisman continues to be a major postcard from her.

Our daughter, Suzanne, went to Spirit in 2011 and this is the journey I and her stepfather Mike took through grief and loss. This book also details the help she gave us from the other side. I began a daily journal a few days after she passed as a way to still talk to her in some way. We spoke to each other daily for all of her days on Earth and it seemed impossible not to continue.

In this book, the narratives in the chapters entitled "Interesting Things," and "A Penny for Her Thoughts" contain some of the journal entries that express the grief, wonder, and joy that Mike and I have experienced through the years. They relate the many ways Spirit can contact you too and help you be ready to receive that communication when the time is right. Finally, I want to tell you that the grief of your loss really can be made manageable and perhaps even turn to joy.

I was a hatha yoga teacher in the Los Angeles area for many years. At the end of every class I had my students lie flat and relax for a few minutes to center their thoughts. Before dismissing class and while lying in this pose of relaxation, I read them something inspirational. The following is one of my favorites. It comes from a letter written in the 1500s, from a Franciscan friar to a grieving friend in need.

I salute you. I am your friend and my love for you goes deep. There is nothing I can give you which you have not, but there is much that while I cannot give it you can take. No heaven can come to us unless our hearts find rest in it today. Take heaven. No peace lies in the future which is not hidden in this present instant. Take peace. The gloom of the world is but a shadow. Behind it, yet within reach is joy. Take joy. There is radiance and glory in darkness, could we but see. And to see, we have only to look. I beseech you to look.

Life is so generous a giver. But we, judging its gifts by their covering, cast them away as ugly or heavy or hard. Remove the covering and you will find beneath it a living splendor, woven of love by wisdom, with power. Welcome it, grasp it, and you touch the angel's hand that brings it to you. Everything we call a trial, a sorrow, or a duty, believe me, that angel's hand is there. The gift is there and the wonder of an overshadowing presence. Your joys, too, be not content with them as joys, they too, conceal diviner gifts. Life is so full of meaning and purpose, so full of beauty beneath its covering, that you will find earth but cloaks your heaven. Courage then to claim it, that is all. But courage you have, and the knowledge that we are pilgrims together, wending through unknown country home.

~Fra Giovanni Giocondo (c.1435–1515), Franciscan friar

And now your ship has come,
and you must needs go.
Deep is your longing for the land of your
memories and the dwelling place of your
greater desires:
and our love would not bind you nor our
needs hold you.

"THE COMING OF THE SHIP"

FROM *THE PROPHET* BY KAHLIL GIBRAN

Suzanne

"You aren't going to die too, are you, Mom?" My eight-year old daughter sat on the end of my bed looking at me with her big, anxious blue-gray eyes, and took hold of my hand on this dreary Southern California morning. It had been the typical April, overcast with dim light and dampness in the air. And a lot of sadness too. My two daughters and I had been given a lot of heartbreaking news in a short period of time, and I did not think I could take any more. My sensitive Suzanne would not leave my side, continually checking on me, trying desperately to cheer me up, afraid that *I* would die. She got into bed with me, and I wrapped her up in my arms while I tried to gain some composure for the children's sake.

We three were in grief from the death of my best friend a few days before, whom I had known since child-hood. Brenda was a treasured "Auntie Mame" to the girls, and she was much loved by all of us. Her death

1

by suicide was devastating. She had lost her six-year-old son to a medical mistake about a year before and was not able to manage her sorrow. The evening before she put the gun to her head, she called me, and we spoke for a very long time about our lives and adventures. She said, "Judi, I don't know if I can go on without Christopher. I try and I try but I just feel like I want to be with him. I want you to know that I love you and the girls very much and I always will. You have been with me all of my life—you have been a sister to me through all of my life."

I said, "Please, please, just hang on tonight. I can only imagine your pain right now. Listen, I'll come over and see you early in the morning. I'll make us some tea and we can talk some more. I'll stay as long as you need me. I promise."

She said, "Okay, I'll see you in the morning." But in the morning Brenda was gone. Losing her son was just too much grief.

To add to our misery, my ex-husband, Robert, who was the father of our two girls, was in the hospital with a very poor prognosis for alcoholism, and the man whom at the time I thought I was going to spend my life with had just left me for a younger woman. Three big emotional hits in a very short period of time had left me a complete wreck. I was in a very deep depression, hardly able to get out of bed or tend to the needs of my children, who, of course, were also trying to process all of these heart-wrenching events.

My ex-husband was an alcoholic in the days when not so much was known about the condition. We didn't think of his drinking as a disease or an addiction but as a choice. I left him and took the girls because of his continued destructive drinking and what it was doing to the family. Life was hard. A divorced woman with children in the 1970s had a difficult time in the best of circumstances, both socially and economically, and we had very little family support. For some time, Robert's family and my family thought I was a bad woman, somehow responsible for his drinking and the breakup of the marriage. My girls were both damaged by our broken home—Suzanne more outwardly so than her more resilient older sister, Jennifer. Of course, no one escapes this kind of damage.

Suzanne's words shook me into the present moment, and I replied while hugging her, "No, Suzanne. I am not going to die, but if I ever do, I will never leave you. I will be with you always."

Her eyes brightened as she grinned at my words and said, "Okay, Mom, and if I ever die, I will never leave you either. We will always be together—we will make a pact." That pact was repeated many times over the years when there was a crisis— and our little family did have quite a few. Little did I know that Suzanne would die before me.

Our Pact

Suzanne died at the age of thirty-nine after a long and difficult illness. This book is about her journey of the Spirit, and how my daughter has kept our pact to be in touch with amazing postcards sent through the veils that are between realms. It is also about our march though grief and loss toward peace and acceptance of this new reality.

Children are songs that your heart sings. And although we love our children in equal measure, we love them differently, and the song Suzanne sings to me is deeply resonant to who I am. We are incredibly close. When she was born and the nurse put this newborn child into my arms, I already knew her. We looked into each other's eyes and I said with deep inner knowledge, "You will teach me more than I will ever be able to teach you." And that she has. I am honored to have been her mother in this life.

She was a sensitive soul, like me. We intuit how others feel, and often, if we're not careful, we will confuse the emotions of others with our own. When small, Suzanne knew when the phone was going to ring and who it was on the other end. She would tell me, "Grandma is calling," or Nancy, or another friend. Then the phone would ring, and she would be right. If I was unhappy or angry with her father, she would immediately act out, mirroring my own feelings even when I tried so hard to mask them. Picking up on the feelings of others and not knowing how to deal with those feelings in a constructive way is hard on a little girl. When she was a young woman living away from home, I would pick up the phone to call her only to find her already on the other end. We did not need the phone to ring. We finished each other's sentences and would laugh so hard at the same jokes and at life's irony that we would collapse in a heap.

Suzanne was physically beautiful: a dancer's body both long-limbed and graceful. In addition, she had a unique and creative soul. Her life, with all of her struggles and triumphs of both mind and body, are worthy of a book of its own. However, this is about her triumph of the Spirit and proof of the afterlife that she has shown through communication with us and with others. It is Suzanne's gift to those who grieve.

Suzanne attended a Waldorf school from preschool through eighth grade in Southern California. Waldorf education, based on the philosophy of Rudolf Steiner, an early 19th century Austrian social reformer, is worldwide and is known for encouraging art, philosophy, and the exploration of the spirit. Suzanne excelled in that environment. At an early age, her high intelligence and art and language abilities were in full force while her talent for classical dance earned her a place in the Joffrey Ballet summer programs in New York City.

After eighth grade, she went to our local high school where she was so bored that they let her take classes at the community college nearby.

Even with her difficulties with depression, anxiety, and sensitivity, my daughter as a young adult amazed me with her ability to be able to be comfortable with people from all walks of life. She wanted to help anyone or anything that was in trouble or discomfort. In many ways my daughter was fearless, with an open heart. When her bipolar disorder was not raging, she could talk to a homeless person with empathy and kindness, wanting to know how she could help. She could also be at home conversing with a friend about architecture, fine art, or classical music. She spent nine of her adult years in San Francisco exploring the alternative music scene, goth clubs, and other music hangouts. She helped to promote bands, wrote for an underground music magazine, and spoke with music producers, musicians, and crew with knowledge and confidence. A gifted artist, she produced paintings and botanic drawings that fill my walls.

I believe her ability to have made all of these far-reaching personal connections in her Earthly life is one of the reasons her Spirit is able to navigate between realms. She is afraid of nothing and no one. I believe she is needed to help me write this book. I hope she and I can be of use to other people who are grieving and allow them to heal even a little bit—to know that loved ones are not far away and communication may be there for the finding.

Nature's first green is gold,
her hardest hue to hold.
Her early leaf's a flower,
but only so an hour.
Then leaf subsides to leaf.
So Eden sank to grief,
So dawn goes down today.
Nothing gold can stay.

"NOTHING GOLD CAN STAY"
FROM NEW HAMPSHIRE,
BY ROBERT FROST

The Long Road Traveled

Suzanne lived alone in San Francisco for close to ten years but struggled with an addiction to pain medication brought on by a serious accidental burn to her arm. This improperly attended burn resulted in a difficult bone infection. After a rape at knifepoint, she added PTSD to her struggles as well as a diagnosis of bipolarity. She needed us and we needed her near. My husband, Mike, and I asked her to come to New York City to live next to us and begin to heal. We had purchased the one-bedroom apartment adjoining our two-bedroom years before, thinking to combine them sometime in the future, so we had a home ready for her. It took some doing for her to leave her beloved San Francisco but she moved in one April day and began to seriously overcome her addiction, cure the bone infection, start difficult therapy, and live a healthier life. The road was not easy or straight but she ultimately prevailed in creating her art, going back to college, and working hard with her therapist and doctors.

Despite the many anxious days and nights of all of us helping her battle her mental and physical struggles, we three also had wonderful times together. We spent good days and nights at our summer home on Long Island. We walked on the beach, swam in the pool, and found solace in nature. Suzanne and I played our favorite game, Scrabble, in which she usually beat me, and she played chess with Mike. She was a shopper for sure, even though she spent many hours just looking at what the world was offering but not buying much. With her long dark hair and dressed in her flowery dresses, velvets, and Dr. Martens shoes, she was a beautiful sight. I see those clothes now in stores or on people in the street and it is her … it is her.

Unfortunately, and unknown to any of us, her body was already damaged beyond repair. She was diagnosed with bronchiectasis, a lung condition where airways are damaged and frequent infections follow, as well as pulmonary hypertension, a form of high blood pressure between the heart and lungs. The progression of this type of hypertensive disease can be slow and hard, usually with heart failure at the end of the journey. There is currently no cure.

Not Allowed to Leave

After undergoing a couple of close brushes with death from complications of her medical issues and surviving them, our daughter was hit with another infection that sent her back to the hospital emergency room on a cold March day. Her lungs and her heart were failing her so she was immediately put into a medically induced coma to see what could be done. For two weeks the expert staff at the New York-Presbyterian ICU worked to save her life. We were told again to be prepared for the worst. Jenn, her best friend from California, her mom, and our family members flew to the city to be by her side; Mike and I were there constantly. We all made sure that she was never alone, day or night. She was always surrounded with love.

Then one morning, as Mike and I met with the doctors, we were told things were not going well and to prepare to lose her. In that moment all of the air in the consulting room vanished. I could not breathe or think or process what the doctors were telling me. All I heard was "lose her." I believe my heart stopped; my life stopped. My hearing dimmed and my eyes could see nothing. Mike shook me and said, "Stop this, come back, she needs you now, we need you here now to be strong for her. I need you." Still, day after day she hung on, and time began to blur.

Early one wet, cold evening I had come home from the hospital exhausted and lay down on our bed. But I suddenly panicked, deeply afraid that Suzanne was now dying and leaving us right then. I sat up in a sweat as if jolted awake by an electric shock and screamed out loud, "No, no, you cannot leave yet! Please, not yet!" Mike came running into the room to calm me down. Hugging me, he said, "You just came home and need to rest—you haven't slept at all. Listen to me, her friends are with her now and I promise we'll go back first thing in the morning." But I could not relax. Instead, I paced around, seeing in my mind her Spirit lifting and leaving us. I had to go back to the hospital and sit with her for a few more hours, stroking her hand and talking to her, telling her I loved her over and over. When dawn broke, she was better, more stable. The following morning, she was finally conscious, wondering what had happened and why we were all crying and so upset. I would like to think that my screaming for her not to leave me brought her back but it doesn't work that way, as her words to me explained.

"Mom," she said, "I need to tell you this. Write it down, this is important." While in that coma with her life literally hanging by a thread, she vividly remembered having to appear before a sort of committee. She stood in front of several seated people who were looking through a large file and discussing her life. Then they told her she could not come yet; she was not finished with her life yet and she had to go back—there was more work to do.

She also told me she heard everything that was being said while she was in that coma. She felt everything done to her by doctors, nurses, and visitors. She remembered me being by her bed, stroking her hand and speaking to her. She wanted this to be known to everyone who came into a hospital room so that both members of the medical field and visitors would be careful of what they did and said while tending a patient under heavy sedation or in an induced coma. It was a plea to be kind and gentle, to watch one's words and physical touch.

Home Again

After almost a month in the hospital in 2010, Suzanne finally came home, just in time for Easter. Now constantly on oxygen, Suzanne found her life becoming smaller and smaller. Her portable oxygen container allowed her to be away from home for only a few short hours until it needed filling again. Even that was too much for her flagging energy. Now mostly confined to her apartment, she discovered that even though her depression was growing, she produced some of her most beautiful botanical art in pen and pencil. She was thoughtful and creative, uncertain of dying but exhausted from living.

She expressed many times her love for us and her appreciation for our constant and unwavering support. The anger she carried through her life was gone, replaced by love.

She lost weight and even though I cooked her favorite meals, she could not bring herself to eat them. I said, "Suzanne, you must eat even a little bit—please, do it for me."

She responded, "Mom, the world does not have any kind of food that tastes good to me now." She sipped smoothies and drank water and I didn't press her. I felt my daughter was slowly dying, and it was breaking my heart.

To see my daughter waste away was the hardest thing I have ever experienced. Certainly, the doctors did not tell us of the likely future. Neither her GP, nor her pulmonologist, nor her cardiologist explained the severity of her illness. Mike and I researched her conditions on the internet and found her life expectancy was a maximum of five years. We looked at each other in shock, and Mike said, "My God, what do we do now?"

I replied, "We love her until she is gone." We cried in each other's arms, for there was nothing else we could do.

Her Passing

Ten months later, Suzanne's heart failed her, and this Earthly life ended for her. Her last ten months at home on oxygen were so hard for her. She told me she could not live this way and if she left, she hoped I would forgive her for leaving. With a broken heart I said, "I will but you have to remember our pact and stay in touch from the other side."

"Okay," she said while holding my hand, "I will. Don't worry, I will always be with you." At the end of a very cold northeastern January at home, she said, "I love you, Mom" and I replied, "I love you too." Those were the last words Suzanne said to me that evening. Early the next morning she drew her last breath, with family and loved ones around her.

Although we knew she was seriously ill and her death was not far off, when it actually came to pass, we were not ready for it. We were not ready, but no one is ever ready for this kind of loss. Whether loss comes from a long illness or a sudden death, for those who are left behind and grieve, the entire world comes to an immediate stop. After the initial impact of Suzanne's death, her stepdad Mike, and I tried to make sense of it. My pain was overwhelming and bone crushing. I twirled in circles, screaming, "I don't know what to do, I don't know how to live now—I cannot live now!" Mike also was struck with the deep grief of losing a stepdaughter he loved as his own while he was also so very worried about me. In my mind I could see Suzanne twirling too, grief-stricken at leaving us. On one hand, she no doubt

was happy to be released from the body that had be-
trayed her, and, on the other hand, I know it was hard
for her to see those who loved her enduring such pain
at her loss.

On one occasion when Suzanne was very ill, I had told
Mike that if she died, he would shortly thereafter bury
me. I knew that she and I were connected by a metaphysical silver cord and if the cord were broken, I could
just lie down and stop breathing. My grandmother did
that when she lost her favorite son to tuberculosis. I
would have done so too had it not been for my love for
Mike, my older daughter Jennifer, the grandkids, and
the knowledge that my death would leave them with a
double measure of grief.

Then It Hit Me ...

Then it truly hit me. I would not hear Suzanne's voice
again or feel her hugs or laugh at her humor or shop
with her in our favorite haunts or walk down the street
with her. My daughter was not physically there. I felt
enormous panic and unbearable pain penetrating my
heart and my solar plexus. For many days my throat
closed up and I felt it difficult to swallow, breathe, or
think. I talked to her Spirit then and saw her in my
mind. I kept telling her I loved her. I could hear her say
she loved me too. I could see her reaching out to me, but

we couldn't touch. I wrote to her and explained what was happening here. I asked her advice on everything. I twirled in circles and wept and wept. For days on end I never left the house. I could not bear to talk to anyone, not even Mike.

I screamed and yelled and howled. I did not sleep, I did not eat, I hardly took in air. Poor Mike didn't get his share of me to help him in his grief as he was heartbroken too. He had lost a beloved daughter, for he was her dad in all the ways a girl needs and loves a dad.

It was hard to believe the world was going on as usual. I resented the sound of laughter and the sight of people going about their daily business while I grieved. How could the sun shine when all I saw was darkness and all I felt was pain? "My daughter died!" I wanted to scream at them. How could others be happy when I was so broken?

All of the things that must happen when a death occurs had to be followed out. Phone calls had to be made, and arrangements as well. It's all a blur now; I don't remember much of those days. Mike and I traveled through time like unseeing ghosts. People arrived from San Francisco, Seattle, Los Angeles, and Oregon—her friends and mine, her aunt, uncle, cousin, sister, brother-in-law, and her niece and nephew. On a very brisk February day, a memorial service was held at our church, St. Bartholomew's Episcopal, here in the city and so many people came that we were overwhelmed with gratitude.

They included her friends, our friends and family, even her doctors, dentist, and physical therapists! The love that poured out for her from seemingly everywhere amazed and comforted us all. I felt her Spirit with us, looking on.

Finding Grace

I soon felt her Spirit again with me, trying to calm me down. I knew she was so much better off now on the spiritual plane, unencumbered by a failing body. But the reality of loss is very heavy when you lose a child no matter the age or how close you were. I felt I had somehow failed to keep her safe and well. I had failed to protect my child—this child so close to my heart, my best friend, the one who knew me the best of anyone.

Sometimes grace is found in the most unusual ways. After Suzanne's death I sought counsel from our rector, Rev. William Tully, at St. Bartholomew's. Although Mike and I are not rule-bound churchgoers, we have enjoyed the sermons and services at our very liberal Episcopalian church. Between my tears I told our rector the only place I currently felt comfortable was in Suzanne's apartment, where I could talk to her, write to her, hear her answers, slow my heartbeat, and calm my soul.

Reverend Tully looked at me with deep understanding and said, "The apartment is a 'thin place' for you."

He went on to say, "A 'thin place' is where the separation of the planes of life and afterlife are very thin, almost transparent." He said, "Allow yourself to heal there." He went on. "There are many such places on Earth and if you are open to unusual opportunities, often wonderful things can happen. You can have feelings of great inner peace, conveyance of long-sought-for answers, and spiritual awakening."

After speaking with him, I found many books and poetry written about these places and I found comfort in reading them. There is much information on thin places to be found in the Celtic traditions. The aparment remains a thin place for me to this day. There is a description about thin places written by the late Harvard theologian, Peter J. Gomes, in his book *The Good Book: Reading the Bible with Mind and Heart*. Here is some of what he says, "There is in Celtic mythology the notion of 'thin places' in the universe, where the visible and the invisible world come into their closest proximity. To seek such places is the vocation of the wise and the good, and those who find them find the clearest communication between the temporal and the eternal. Monasteries and holy places were meant to be founded at such spots to increase the likelihood of a transcendental communication."[1]

---

1 Peter J. Gomes, *The Good Book: Reading the Bible with Mind and Heart*, chapter 10, "The Bible and Suffering."

It was such a blessing to find out about these thin places. Suzanne herself often said she thought her apartment was a place where she felt grace and the Spirits of others. I also feel that loved ones come back to visit the places where they were comfortable and were loved. If we can sit and listen with love and open hearts, we will feel their presence with us.

Trying to Move Forward

For the first few years after Suzanne's move to Spirit, I believe that 90 percent of my thoughts were with my daughter and about her. Even if I were sitting with friends, or watching a film, attending a party, or talking with others, I really was not present. I was with Suzanne.

I talked to her constantly, wrote to her every day, and let her answers guide me. As I silently heard my daughter's familiar voice, she guided me as to how I was to give away some of the things she treasured and to whom. These precious treasures included ancient books, antique teacups, some of her drawings and artwork, jewelry, and photos of people she loved.

Over time, very slowly and painfully, I began to spend more and more time in the present.

I talked to healers who delicately reminded me that both Suzanne and I needed to get on with the business we had at hand, with me here and her there. One healer said, "You need to move the silver cord that binds you up to your heart chakra from where it is in your solar plexus. If it stays where it is, neither of you will be able to move forward. You know you both have work to do on your own planes of existence." The healer told me not to worry—I could stay attached but move forward with love and good health. With deep meditation I tried to do just that. I began to adapt to this new reality of her existence on a different plane instead of hugs and phone calls. I do this both for Suzanne and for the family I love, who is here.

My days and nights are not so painful now and I can find joy and have days without a thought of sadness, but instead have thoughts of gratitude for my daughter's life and her continued presence in Spirit. You can do the same for yourself and your loved ones. I have realized it can be a selfish thing to spend too much time in heavy grief. Just knowing Spirit is often near allows the healing to begin and to continue. I finally understand a heart broken by loss will never completely heal. The hole in the heart becomes less painful , but it is always there. When we sustain a wound so deep, there always remains a sensitive scar.

I met a lovely woman during our travels who during our talks revealed she had lost her nineteen-year-old son thirty-five years before and she still missed him.

She said now and then the scar is touched by a memory or a word and it is a hard blow. She still talks to him daily and feels his presence around her from time to time. But she can smile now and go on with her life. She sees her son welcoming in other members of the family as they too leave this realm.

The key is to remember with joy and to celebrate the lives our loved ones were given and to remember that the loss is ours, not theirs. They are quite happy to be free from the hard school of life on Earth. The good news is the fact that the unhealed part of our hearts enables us to feel deep compassion for others who are coping with loss. So in that way loss can be a gift to humanity. We can help one another with love and understanding.

So yes, time does heal. But it does not have to heal in a way that locks you away from your loved one. We must go on and live our lives, but it does not mean that our loved ones are no longer an active presence on our journey. My daughter is with me when I have need of her or when she wishes to be heard. I believe the Spirit of your loved ones are often near you too.

Suzanne has never really left us. Her sensitive, intelligent, and mischievous spirit is very present in my daily life. Her postcards—or messages—have come in so many different ways. Mike and I have witnessed phenomena that are not explainable. Suzanne has also constantly directed us to a postcard in the form of a found penny when she wishes to make herself known. This occurs wherever we may happen to be in the world. And her ability to invade our dreams with meaning is astonishing. Every day I talk to her and when she is near, I hear her voice in my head providing me with insight and direction. The tone of her voice is precisely hers, as is the style, logic, and unique brand of humor with which she presents her communication.

This does not mean my grief is over or anyone's grief is ever completely over. But because I know her Spirit is near me, the pain of grief is manageable. Sometimes I still cry and howl and miss her physical presence, but since I know she is out of both emotional and physical pain while joyfully doing the work she was meant to do on the next plane of existence, I can laugh with her at memories and celebrate the life she experienced here on Earth. You can do the same.

I hope in this telling you find healing from the loss of a child or a loved one and know those loved ones are not so far away, and that they may be leaving you postcards in the form of unexplained phemonena, or a message in the form of a special talisman like our found penny too.

For life and death are one,
even as the river and the sea are
one.

"ON DEATH"

FROM *THE PROPHET*

BY KAHLIL GIBRAN

Interesting Things

I had the idea for this book for a while but found it too emotionally difficult to write. So I kept putting it off, ideas swimming in my head but not a single page organized. I was thinking about the passage of time one morning in my bathroom while I was looking though a makeup drawer that was situated on the opposite wall from a glass shelf. Suddenly, the heavy silver-framed clock sitting on the shelf crashed to the tile floor at my feet. It landed with an awful thud, but the clock and I were unharmed. Shaken, I said, "Okay, okay, Suzanne, yes, time *is* flying by." I promptly started to write.

Suzanne has reached out to us in so many ways since her transition to Spirit, just as we promised each other in our "pact" to stay in touch in the afterlife. Shortly after her death so many unexplainable, interesting things began to happen and still do. I call these unexplainable things postcards from my daughter.

If you think about how your loved ones would call your attention while on Earth, they will likely use that method on the next plane of existence. A favorite song may be played at the right moment, or you may have a wisp of a familiar scent, see a favorite bird or animal acting oddly, or solid articles, such as small pieces of clothing or your glasses may seem to move around a bit. You may have thought you lost your keys, only to find them in the most unlikely place where you would never have put them, or they may turn up in exactly the place you just looked but they weren't there before. Your attention may be constantly drawn to an object, like a penny, a certain flower or bird and you realize in the moment of finding or seeing that object you also feel your loved one. Sometimes even in the absence of anything tangible you may just feel the presence of Spirit, calming you and assuring you all is well. Leave your heart and mind open. Your love for each other does not stop manifesting itself because of death. It goes on forever.

I am no stranger to the ways those who have passed can use to reach out to us. The way contact is made certainly seems to reflect who they were in life. Our close friend Deb loved nature and was particularly drawn to butterflies. Deb died way too young of a rare cancer. Her many friends and family were shocked and shaken by the loss. One afternoon, just before her passing, her father sat by her side, not wanting her to leave him. Deb said to him, "Look for me, Dad. I am going to be the butterfly that comes to visit you." Her dad was an avid gardener so a few days after her transition to Spirit, he was working in his garden when a large butterfly flew right to his shoulder and stayed with him all afternoon. He knew it was Deb by her energy and he felt deeply soothed. He was visited by many such butterflies for many months. When we see a friendly one now, we salute her.

Our sister-in-law, Sophia, contracted cancer and died a few months before Suzanne. Her husband and grown children were unusually close to her, and her death was an extremely difficult loss. Her son, Kevin, was driving in heavy traffic with his two small boys a week or so after her death, talking with them about their beloved *Bhabha*, their word for grandmother. He wondered out loud, "Where are you now, Mom?" Just then a large car swerved in front of him, bringing him to alertness. He stared at the vanity license plate, which read BHABHA. He had his answer. She was with them.

My father's death from a stroke hit my mother very hard. He was only sixty and they were just beginning to enjoy the latter stages of their lives after raising four children. At his death, my mother was inconsolable for weeks on end. One night, lying awake in bed restless and unable to sleep because of her sorrow, she saw a light at the doorway of her room. This frightened her and she closed her eyes, unable to move. Through closed eyes she saw the light move closer and then felt a tremendous surge of energy full of love. This energy enveloped her body like a loving hug and kiss. She could hear a whisper from my dad telling her not to cry anymore for he would be there for her. The energy and light slowly faded away. This visit calmed her and started her on the road to healing.

Soon after Suzanne's death, both Mike and I became aware of her presence. Even in our deepest grief when life seemed no longer real and we walked through our days and our nights as though we were wrapped in gauze, we could feel her with us. My mantra became "I love you, Suzanne" and I heard back "I love you, Mom." It still is my mantra. I must say it at least a hundred times a day and I hear her saying it her back to me.

As I mentioned earlier, Suzanne was always a mischievous person with a wicked sense of humor. She loved to stir things up a bit. I am a neat freak and she was not, to put it mildly. I need people and things to be on time and organized so I can think clearly, and she loved an unorganized chaos. She had no idea of how long a minute is or how to hang up her clothes. She found this difference between us humorous and we did often laugh about it. So, of course, she continued to do in the afterlife what she did while she was here on Earth. Although her clothes were no longer an issue, other things began to happen.

While here, she would often tilt the art on my walls and reset my clocks to the wrong time just to make me crazy. After her death, my pictures on the wall began to always be on a slant no matter how much I straightened them, and my clocks are now always off a few minutes but the correct time is never displayed on any of them. Fixing the pictures over and over and resetting the clocks make me smile, and we acknowledge her presence in the house. I am still fixing pictures and resetting clocks, particularly after Mike and I have been talking about her. In fact, pictures have fallen completely off the wall with a resounding thud. There is never any damage—we just say, "Okay. Hi, Suzanne."

Questions

One morning shortly after Suzanne left us, I was deep in grief and sort of wandering around the apartment, unable to focus on anything. I wished I would see her suddenly bursting through our front door like she always did, yelling out, "Anybody home?" I had some shopping to do and I was on my way to some of her favorite places. The bookstore, the art shop, and a shoe store for new winter shoes were on my list and I so much wanted her with me. Standing in my bathroom with tears flooding my eyes, I opened the mirrored cabinet and was just about to reach for an item, when suddenly an eye cream container flew out of the cabinet at eye level, then made a left-hand turn, and hit the wall precisely at the light switch, turning off the light. There I stood in shocked darkness! She was there, wanting me to stop crying. I did.

That was just the beginning. I wanted to know more. I wanted to find a medium.

Looking for a Medium

I wanted to find a medium because both Mike and I had psychic friends but did not know any mediums. A person with psychic abilities can sense things about the future and the past, but mediums are gifted people who can communicate from one plane of existence to another. A gifted person can have both abilities. Suzanne had a great interest in mediums so I knew if I found the right one, she could contact me through them. I am also aware this area of spirituality can be easily misused so I am a healthy skeptic until proven otherwise. But how to find an honest and caring medium? Well, here is what happened.

About a year after Suzanne's death, many people posted to her Facebook memorial page and to my page with sweet thoughts and memories, all celebrating Suzanne's complicated and amazing life. The following post was very special and started Mike and me on the path to healing and communicating with Suzanne through the use of mediums.

Daria and Nell

I received a note from Suzanne's school chum Daria, who lives in Southern California. She wrote of a visit she had had from Suzanne and introduced me to a marvelous medium named Nell:

Judith, you have been so much in my thoughts. Just know I'm thinking of you and sending you much love. Suzanne has been on my mind so much too. Please don't think I am crazy, but I'd like to tell you a story about a recent "visit" from Suzanne. A small group of moms from my kid's school have been meeting fairly regularly on Fridays after school—sort of like a playdate for our kids and a much-needed social time for us moms. Last Friday the meeting took place at Nell's house and I was the first one there. She was looking at me oddly and kept glancing over at me, but I just thought she was distracted.

After an hour or so into our gathering, Nell wanted to read an angel card for each of us. Angel cards are like tarot cards but have messages from angels. This was odd as Nell has never done this except in private conversation. Nell is an unbelievably spiritually gifted medium who can see and hear Spirits and also pick up on energy and auras.

She went around the group, and one by one had the person pull an angel card from the deck. Then she would read it and explain the message and what she heard/felt about it in detail. When it came to my turn, I pulled a card and handed it to her. She said "Oh, uh-huh," and handed it back to me to read. She then said, "You know who this is, right?"

As I read it and nodded yes, I absolutely knew. The angel card I picked was the Sonya card, here, in short, is what it said: "I bring you this message from your deceased loved one: 'I am happy, at peace, and I love you very much. Please don't worry about me.'

"Your heart has been heavy with grief, and I am here to reassure you. I am a guardian angel to your deceased loved one, and I want you to know that there is no reason for you to worry. Your loved one is very happy and has adjusted to the transition very well."

"You and your loved one still share great love between your souls. That love could never die! Although you miss your loved one's physical presence, you have already connected spiritually in your dreams, as well as through feeling, hearing, smelling, or seeing your loved one's essence. Your loved one is as alive as you are—even more alive

in many ways. Relieved of earthly cares and bodily pains, your loved one is freer and happier than ever. As soon as you complete your life's purpose and it is your time to make the transition, you will be reunited in each other's arms. In the meantime, please know that your loved one is with you often, and that the angels surround you constantly."

Nell then said to me, "Well, you didn't walk in alone, that's for sure." Later she told me she was so surprised when I walked in with a Spirit next to me, she told her (the spirit) she didn't want to deal with her right now. She said she was next to me the whole time, and when I pulled the angel card, the spirit said, "She will know who it is from." I was stunned.

I finally was able to visit with Nell later in the week. I didn't tell her anything about Suzanne (not even her name), just said I thought it was my friend who had passed last year, waiting to make sure it was her and to get a better validation. Nell pulled three angel cards and said that they weren't for me at all. There was a very strong motherly sort of feeling with the cards and the spirit. She asked if my friend's name was "Suzy." She said the card reading was more for Suzy's mother.

Nell continued to say Suzanne knows her mom blames herself very much for how her daughter's life turned out, but also knows her mom only wanted *the best for her and was in constant pursuit of that. She knows her mom blames herself for so many things—like, "if I had only done this … or if I had only done that … then things would have been differ- ent." And she knows her mom feels Suzanne would have had a family of her own (that she feels they both missed out on). She would not have gotten sick. But Suzanne wanted her mom to know none of that was her mom's fault. She'd made the choice to not have kids. She'd chosen her lifestyle to be the way it was. What happened in her life was her choice, and what happened was ultimately meant to be.*

She also said her mom was punishing herself. Su- zanne wants her mom to realize it wasn't her fault. She wants nothing more than to have her find all the good in life, it's not too late at all, and her mom is too caught up in the "minutia" (her exact word) of the day-to-day life. She wants her to be happy. She also mentioned she's with her mom all the time.

I made sure it was okay to share this with you, and Nell said absolutely, and that Suzanne wanted me to be in contact with you and you could call Nell at any time because Suzanne had more to say.

This posting from Daria was such a gift to me. I absolutely planned to speak directly to Nell. Now, I began to be open to and aware of messages from my daughter.

Roses

Roses were among my daughter's favorite flowers, and the scent of roses from candles, soaps, or incense filled her home and scented her body. She loved to dry roses and hang them in her apartment until they crumpled from age. One afternoon, Mike and I were off to an early movie and stopped at a favorite restaurant that was decorated in a French bistro manner with old posters and a bar of beautifully carved wood. Since we were early, we decided to have a glass of wine before dinner at the unoccupied bar and almost-empty bistro.

As we sat there, we talked about how much Suzanne loved the decor of this place when all of a sudden Mike said, "I smell roses!" I looked at him and realized I could smell the scent of roses too.

I replied, "So do I—her favorite scent!"

Mike, with a grin, said, "The kid is here with us today."

The beautiful delicate odor of roses filled us with the joy of her presence and then was gone. Laughing out loud, we again looked around the bistro and it was truly empty. She was telling us, "Yes, I am here."

So much of our emotional memory is connected to and set off by a favorite scent. Just think of how you feel when you smell the aroma of your favorite dinner cooking, or of chocolate chip cookies baking.

Spirit can use these emotional connections to contact you. A scent that brings up sudden memories of a loved one, like the fragrance of a favorite perfume, or of pipe tobacco, even the smell of cigarettes, is often manifested by Spirit as a hello message. These moments are wonderful to have. Be aware of the scents around you, particularly when you are alone, quiet, and thoughtful.

Spiritual Words

Mike was recovering from a surgery due to diverticulitis and a perforated intestine. It was a very long and hard operation with a difficult recovery. And he wasn't yet done, for he was scheduled for another operation three months later to reconnect the bowel. There was a lot of pain and discomfort for him and wild worry for me. While he was home recuperating he told me of the following amazing visit from Suzanne.

One afternoon after having a nap in the bedroom, he got up and rushed into the den where I was reading quietly. He excitedly said, "Listen to this! I have to tell you right now. All of a sudden, I was awakened by a huge noise like a big bang. It scared me half to death! I sat up in bed and looked over to the bedroom entrance, where I thought the noise had come from, and honest to God, I saw a whirling ball of light moving toward me.

It actually came to me and then entered my body near my belly button where my wound is, then moved down to my feet and slowly back up to my heart. I felt as though my entire body were being lifted off the bed with energy and light. I had goose bumps! I know that light was Suzanne—it was her."

I said, "Michael she came to help you to heal. You need to remember this!"

He replied, "But that's not all. Listen to what she told me—I hope I put this just like she did. She said, 'Life is just one continuing energy and time is not linear—all is together. All life is interconnected and continuing. We have all been together so many times before and will be again if we choose. There is great beauty and peace in the other dimensions and good work to do for the souls here. I am part of that, and you and Mom are part of that even though you are still there. To love each other is the most important thing. It is important to leave whatever is in the past in the past, go forward, do not wait, do not hesitate, go forward now.'"

I immediately got pen and paper and wrote it down as Mike relayed it to me.

We have had other such spiritual messages from Suzanne, allowing us to understand more about life and death and more about what it all means. Try to be aware of your thoughts when you are totally relaxed and your mind is open. You can receive such messages too.

Doctor in the House

It was flu season in the Northeast, and Mike and I had not been feeling so great and had been to the family doctor for this and that ailment. One weekend evening, Mike was acting and feeling odd and we could not figure out what to do about his weird symptoms. Completely befuddled, I turned my mind and heart to Suzanne to ask what to do. I told her, "Suzanne, Mike is not feeling well. His heart is racing, and he has the shakes. It could be a sugar thing or atrial fibrillation, or I don't know what. I made him a shake with banana and apple and a little potassium, and now he is lying down again. This heart thing is very scary, as you know. You two might have a lot of fun together but I cannot bear the thought of losing him. See what you can do—tell me what to do."

I sat on the sofa and kept my heart open and my mind quiet so I could hear her. After a few minutes, I heard her remind me of an important thing. "Mom," Suzanne told me, "don't you remember when I was given a steroid for a herniated disk and I decided I didn't need them any-more and just stopped them? How crazy I got? More than usual? He has a reaction to coming off the steroid so quickly." I chuckled at that memory, thought about it, and, yes, our internist had given him steroids for an inner ear inflammation that had developed after a cold. His ears had felt better, so he'd decided to just quit taking them abruptly. Steroids are powerful drugs and you cannot stop them quickly or you can have a serious physical and mental reaction—just like the one he was having. I turned to Mike and said, "I have the answer—Suzanne just told me."

Spirit can give you guidance if you just sit and ask and listen. Keep your heart open to messages and help will come.

The Power of Birthdays

Suzanne's birthday is full of memories for me. This is the marvelous day I gave life to this child, the first day I held her and felt the deepest love a woman can feel. So when she shows up in Spirit form for me, or for Mike, or her friends on or near that day, it lifts my heart and drives home the fact she is checking in on all of us and making herself known—if we have the eyes to see and the ears to hear.

Suzanne's best school chum, Daria, has a birthday a few days before hers, and when they were children they often celebrated together. I think this story was a gift for Daria for her birthday.

Daria left me this private message on my Facebook page after Suzanne's birthday in 2012, one year after her death. On a day of mixed memories centered on her life and passing, this message was exactly what I needed to hear. It's an example of my daughter's sense of humor and love for her friend.

Daria relates: "On Suzanne's birthday, she was on my mind. I was home alone with my daughter and the doorbell starting ringing. It's not one of those old ring, ring, ring doorbells, but sounds newer and more like bells. What was weird was it was ringing like someone was playing a song. I immediately got up and checked the door, and no one was there, nor was anyone walking away down the walkway. I stood there, listening. My daughter came over to me and we were kind of shocked and amazed at what we were hearing. I called out loud, 'Is there someone there? Is there someone playing a song for us?' and then the doorbell immediately stopped ringing. I definitely think Suzanne was giving me her own birthday gift."

Of course, for some people, birthdays are no big deal. For Suzanne it was a very big deal and needed to be acknowledged. We still celebrate her birthday and acknowledge her life. Mike usually stays up later than I do to read in the room that once was her bedroom. One year, on the night before her birthday, May 20, Mike and I talked about how we would celebrate the next day. I went to bed and Mike stayed up to watch a movie.

In the morning over coffee, he told me the following story: "You know, I leave the hall light on after you go to bed. Well, in the middle of the movie, that light suddenly began to vibrate and flash like a maniac, off and on, lighter and darker. The bulb was doing a manic flash dance. I thought, *Suzanne.* So I looked at the clock and it was 12:23 a.m. on May 20. And then the light just stopped!" Not only was Mike noting Suzanne's birthday but also her favorite number: twenty-three. We both laughed and toasted her with our coffee. The bulb returned to normal and has been normal ever since. But we do keep an eye on it!

Birthdays are particularly powerful dates for Spirit to be present. A date is just a date but certainly our thoughts, and probably theirs, are focused on the date that they entered the Earth. Celebrate those birthdays with joy, cake, and a candle—a visit may ensue.

Traveling Along

We have found that Suzanne somehow always makes her presence known when we are on a trip. We are relaxed and full of good cheer and it is easy for her to visit.

Mike and I traveled to Oregon late one June to celebrate the one hundredth birthday of my children's paternal grandmother. Grandma Margo was quite a force in Jennifer and Suzanne's lives. Suzanne always loved and respected her grandmother's German discipline and frugality, having none of those traits herself. I felt sure we would hear from Suzanne on this trip. And after finding our postcard penny under the seat in the preboarding area of the Denver airport, I was sure of it.

In 1867, William Henry Seward, then secretary of state, purchased Alaska from Russia for $7 million. It was considered a bad deal, or a "folly" at the time, until gold and other natural resources were discovered there. What a wonderful folly it has turned out to be.

Since we were so close to Alaska, we decided to travel on after the party, take a cruise on a small ship that travels up the inner passage from Vancouver to Anchorage along several small and quaint port cities, and see some of this folly of Mr. Seward.

On this trip, Suzanne made her presence known in several exciting ways.

Suzanne had a love for ravens and crows. She admired their intelligence and their beauty. It seemed whenever or wherever Mike and I travel, a crow or a raven is either following us or waiting for us. Just one, always posed on a lamppost, or a tree branch, or hopping along in front of us. Mike and I feel it is her way of having her Spirit come along. Just when we'd be talking about her, one would appear. "Hi, Suzanne," we would say, and the crow would just look at us, hop back and forth, and hang about for a while.

Alaska was no different.

We liked to sit or stand at the back of the small cruise boat to observe the Alaskan beauty. In one port Mike told me of an unusual visit from Suzanne. He was standing at the back all alone, watching the seabirds and the bald eagles skimming by when all of a sudden out of absolutely nowhere a raven came straight for him and veered off at the very last minute. It really shook him up. There were no other ravens around and no other people in the back of the boat. "Suzanne," he said. "I felt it was Suzanne. She looked me right in the eye. It was her vibration. I felt my energy lift and the hair on the back of my head rose right up."

The cruise made a stop in the town of Juneau. There is a tram in Juneau that goes up to the top of a beautiful mountain with hiking trails. We decided to take the tram and do a little hiking to see what we could find. The trail begins in an old-growth forest and rises into a meadow and finally ends at a high elevation with short trees and bushes. It was a gorgeous day with blue skies and clear Alaskan air and a soft pine scent. Mike is stronger than I am, so I took advantage of a rest stop at a sort of overlook that was surrounded by an old rustic wooden barrier, while he continued walking up before joining me on the way down.

This site presented a perfect photo op. I walked to the edge of the wood barrier and admired the view, then looked down to the wood fence where I had stopped to rest and placed my hand. In the wood, exactly where I had laid my hand down, was a carved heart and next to it the letters *SJ*. I took a sharp breath and blinked my eyes. They were her initials: Suzanne Jones. I felt her energy soar through me when I saw and touched those initials and the heart. There were a lot of carvings on the wood at other places, but somehow Suzanne had guided me to the spot with her *SJ* initials and a heart. I saw Mike coming down the trail and yelled to him, "Mike, Mike, come and see this!" Our grins were ear to ear as we practically floated back to the tram.

If your loved one liked or wished to travel while on Earth, you may find messages while on trips of your own, if you are open, relaxed, and aware enough to receive the postcards along the way.

The Power of Music

Mike and I visited Skagway while on the Alaskan cruise. It is home to maybe a thousand people year-round. The stores have been preserved from the time of the gold rush, and the town is now part of the Klondike Gold Rush National Historical Park. While strolling through Skagway with other tourists from the cruise, checking out the architecture, I heard a raven making a lot of noise. "Hey, look at this crazy bird," I said to Mike. We both stopped to watch it. It was on the roof across the street, marching up and down and screaming its head off. I reached into my bag to find my phone to take a picture. When I pulled out my phone, somehow the music app was activated, (which I really never use) and the song being broadcast was "Suzanne" by Journey, one of my daughter's favorite bands. We stood there, mouths open, listening to the song while the raven danced on the roof across the street. Suzanne, tickling the hair on our heads, was having a great time. At the end of the song, the bird flew off and we gathered ourselves together to ponder Suzanne's ability to talk to us and to travel with us.

At home one cold and dreary December day, while sorting through closets, I saw some of her things and felt her loss so much I posted on my Facebook page that I really missed her. Daria saw my post and sent me a heart icon. A few hours later, she sent me another private post. She wrote, "I have to share this. After I posted to your status, you were heavy on my mind and then I got in my car to run a quick errand. The radio was blaring and the song playing was "I Love You, Suzanne" by Lou Reed. I've never heard that song before and OMG when is that song ever played on the radio? I was so moved, it made me tear up and I'm still in awe. You and I both know from past experiences it was Suzanne giving a message to you and to me."

Of course, I immediately felt much better, knowing that Suzanne was present, working communication through others who are open to receiving it.

Music is a perfect device for Spirit to play with us and make contact. We just need to listen. Like a sudden whiff of a favorite scent, favorite songs can pop up at just the right moment to indicate that Spirit is near and is checking in with us.

Electronic Communication

One winter morning, I woke up immediately, thinking about my youngest daughter and what she had meant to me and how she had impacted my life. It was five-thirty in the morning, early even for me, and after rising, I went to the den where I keep my phone to check messages, hoping nothing would be there about our ailing grandma. After pressing my iPhone to activate it, a large black *S* covered my screen. I blinked a few times in amazement and shook my head and looked again, while the large black *S* slowly faded away. Suzanne's grandmother did not have much time left here on Earth, and I had asked Suzanne the night before to help her in the transition if at all possible. I felt strongly this was Suzanne's answer and I could rely on her to do what she could. I began to relax from this worrisome burden— that her grandmother would be frightened at the time of her passing not to have Suzanne at hand when she needed her granddaughter.

Mike is a student of history and, as we are making history every moment these days, he always checks his phone in the morning for new happenings in the world.

It was near Christmas, always a tense and emotion-filled time for both the living and for those who have passed as they watch us grieve for their loss.

On his phone, to his surprise, there was a garbled text message that looked oddly like the random letter of *M* with *Mom* or *mom* embedded in it. Mike said, "Suzanne!" and rushed to the kitchen, where I was making my coffee, to show it to me. I took a photo of it and some of the letters are shown here:

Mmm.mmmm.non.Mom
Mmmmmm n n M. M. Mom
Mom. M mm mm

Both in life and in Spirit I am always *Mom*, not *Mother*, not *Mommy*, just *Mom* and sometimes to be silly, *Mom, Mom, Mom*, over and over again.

The night before, Mike and I had been sharing stories of Christmases spent with Suzanne, and I was full of her memories and yearning for my unique daughter. A text message in the morning is a wonderful thing.

Jack is a musician Suzanne met while living in San Francisco. Jack became one of Suzanne's favorite people in the world. They were great buddies and she thought of him as a long-lost brother. They continued to be in close touch after she moved to New

York City, with Jack even coming to stay with her for a few days while she was recovering from a delicate spinal surgery. She had trouble wearing shoes then, and Jack, being a gallant, big, strong, and tall guy, pretty much carried her around the city on that visit. The morning she died, Jack called me to make sure it was the truth—that she had truly passed. He said he'd received a phone call from her cell number. There was no message—the call had been placed a short time after she'd passed. When he was told by her other friends in San Francisco that she was gone, he refused to believe it, showing everyone the call log on his phone that indicated the call had been sent after she had died. No one had used her phone that morning. Except, apparently, Suzanne.

Sometimes even now, when I see, in written form, the year 2011 for any reason, I immediately begin to go down a dangerous rabbit hole. The year 2011 is the year of her passing. If I see any date in any written work, my mind begins the calculation of whether she was with us then or not. It is my touchstone of sorts—it's often a painful one.

One afternoon at home not so long ago, I began to go down the rabbit hole again. This was set off by a strong memory trigger of the sight of her medical records in my files. They were dated 2010 when she was so ill. *2010*, I thought—*it's only a few months later and she is physically gone.* So, in my tears I heard her saying, "Mom, you can't focus on a date. I am always with you no matter what. The date is just a date in time. You have to accept that I am here. I am here with you." I began to breathe deeply and to focus on the amazing fact she really is always with me.

At my computer an hour later, I saw that my email was off-line for some reason. I reset the mail and came up with an email notification from Facebook with a link to a page where I was tagged. Curious, I clicked on the page. It was from Suzanne's friend Brian in San Francisco. It was a post from May 20, 2011—her birthdate in the year of her passing. He had a picture of a Memento Mori he was wearing to remember her and other friends who had also passed. Thinking this was odd, I looked at my mailbox and saw my mail was somehow stuck on the same date, with mail from a number of people celebrating her memory. I reread each of those messages and remembered how much Suzanne was and is loved. My heart swelled for my daughter and her ability to do things to help me heal.

The study of metaphysics tells us that Spirit is electricity and therefore our smartphones and computers can be lots of fun for Spirit to use to communicate. Pay attention to the odd things that happen electronically. There are no coincidences.

Bringing Comfort

Mike takes a yearly sailing trip with his best buddy, Dennis, on Dennis's beautiful sailboat. The two of them move his boat from its winter dock in Brooklyn all the way out to the end of Long Island, where it stays for the summer. This requires sailing down the unpredictable East River and on to the Long Island Sound, with some open ocean involved. The course is also heavily trafficked by commercial boats and big fishing vessels. The first day is an all-day and all-night sail. All through the night the two of them go on the wine-dark sea, and I always worry about their safety when there is an all-night sail. We are all getting a bit older, and we're not as strong or alert as we once were.

To make matters worse, even though the tide was right (a sailor's necessity), the weathermen had predicted a storm. The wind was up and the weather was rough when Mike and Dennis left port. So I asked Suzanne, "Please watch over them if you can. I won't sleep tonight." In the morning I received a text from Mike saying they had arrived safely in port after a very stormy and difficult night. He wrote: "Guess the name of the boat next to us in port? *The Suzanne!*" When he called me later, we both laughed, and I thanked her for watching out for them, once again finding comfort in her closeness and her communication methods.

Suzanne's friend Jack and several of her other friends from San Francisco came to her funeral service at St. Bartholomew's in New York. After the service was over, and we had all gathered together in one of Suzanne's favorite French bistros, Jack came to me and said, "During the service I looked up and was sure I saw a glimpse of Suzanne smiling at us from a higher balcony. Then she was gone. Later, when people were leaving, I asked one of the clergies, 'How would you get to that balcony?' and the clergyman told me 'It is impossible—there are no stairs to reach that balcony. It is purely decorative.'"

Jack is absolutely positive he saw Suzanne there; he felt her energy and recognized that smile. If anyone could recognize her in any form, it would be Jack. He knew she was pleased to see so many friends among the gathering. This telling sparked joy and comfort both to Jack and to Mike and me and eased our grief.

Early one morning, I slowly opened my closed eyes to dim light, aware that it was about six o'clock in the morning. I was thinking how particularly nice it was in bed that morning with Mike, so cozy and peaceful. I felt Suzanne next to me. I felt the warmth of her body, snug against mine, I could smell the fragrance of roses in her hair. I had a vision of the three of us, resting and contented. It was such a warm, happy, and relaxed feeling. I felt the bed lighten and her presence gently leave me, so I turned and cuddled with Mike for another hour of sleep.

Later, when we were both awake and preparing breakfast, he asked me if I had dreamed of Suzanne. Startled,
because I hadn't had a chance to tell him my story yet,
I wondered why he wanted to know. He replied, "I woke
about six o'clock and while lying on my side next to you,
I thought I saw her, out of the corner of my eye, get up
from your side of the bed, and leave!" He saw her and I
felt her. This is wonderful, joyful healing stuff.

On New Year's morning a year after her death, I found
Suzanne's journal while going through some other things.
I opened it and my eye was caught by a certain date. On
January 1, 2011, she had written, "I do not feel well at all,
something is wrong. I think I am going to die." This was
a knife through my heart. I doubled over in pain after
reading this sentence. I once again howled with sorrow,
and for a few minutes I could not catch my breath. She
knew death was close. Why had she not shared this with
anyone? We knew she was not feeling well but she didn't
say how terribly unwell she was, nor confide what her
fears were. Maybe it was because of her dislike of hospitals, after having been in them so often. And I know
she was careful not to worry us further. So she suffered
her pain and fear in quiet silence. I was physically sick at
the thought of my daughter all alone with her intuitive
knowledge that her body was failing her.

After mulling about this all morning and calming
down somewhat, I needed to prepare lunch. We have a

persnickety gas stove that doesn't always work, but this time I could not get any of the burners to catch fire. I must have tried twenty-three times, becoming more and more frustrated. Then I realized she was present—she was beside me. "Suzanne," I said, "don't worry. I am going to be fine. Please, let me light the burner and get this meal made. You need to stop blowing it out!" The next time, it lit. Again, she'd moved me from tears to smiles She has done this trick often since then, and once I acknowledge her presence and her love, the stove will always light. We have had it checked by repairmen many times and they swear nothing is physically wrong with it.

Sometimes things happen that cause comfort and love. They are inexplicable assurances that our loved ones are not far away. If you knew Suzanne in life, you would understand her playfulness. If you too look for ways in which your loved ones helped to comfort you or had fun in life, they will no doubt also do so in Spirit.

Positive Ions

Suzanne loved thunderstorms and wild weather. The eastern storms with the positive ions and cracks of thunder and lightning delighted her because we had them so rarely in California where she had grown up.

Hurricane Sandy hit the East Coast in October of 2012. Our home in Manhattan is perched high above the major FDR Drive and looks over the East River in a pretty safe place. We can see a portion of the highway looking to the south toward the United Nations building. That day, we watched through our windows and standing on the balcony as the howling wind became stronger, the trees on our quiet street bending like never before with autumn leaves, and small tree branches and other detritus flying. The water rose higher and higher against the banks of the East River until we could see it breached the FDR drive. It was a dark, eerie scene as you looked south when the police closed the normally busy highway to traffic. I thought that Suzanne would love the drama of this storm and would be with us for it.

I love storms too. Thus, fascinated by the storm's intensity, I went several times out onto the balcony to witness this act of nature. Each time I looked, the wind had increased, the noise of the storm was louder, and the water had risen higher and higher in the river and onto the highway. As the storm became more and more intense, the ions in the air became stronger and more exhilarating. Just her kind of weather! Then on one trip outside, I saw a movement of feathers to my right in the dim light. Perched on a plant hanger attached to the balcony wall on its furthest recess was a water-soaked, coal-black pigeon with golden eyes.

I am not a particular fan of pigeons but this one was unique. I shooed him away with my arms, but he absolutely would not move. I walked straight up to him and yelled, but he did nothing but stare at me with those golden eyes. That pigeon was not going anywhere. I then had a funny feeling in my solar plexus. It hit me that this was not some ordinary pigeon. I said to him, "Who are you with, anyway?" There was no answer except a ruffling of feathers as he stared into my eyes. "Okay," I said, and let him be.

I have never seen such a beautiful pigeon in my life, and I have seen quite a few in this city. All night I checked on him as he huddled there, safe from the fury of the storm, with leaves and small bits of branches landing on the balcony all around him, his amber eyes looking at me, glowing in the darkness. In the morning he was gone, not to return. I do believe Suzanne enjoyed that storm. Crows and ravens were her favorite birds, but I guess if you cannot find a willing crow or raven, a black pigeon will do.

On another evening we had more thunderstorms, and I just felt she was with us that night too. On PBS there was a special broadcast of songs by Carole King and James Taylor. Although I love both of those artists, I was steeling myself because it was announced that James Taylor was going to sing the Leonard Cohen song "Suzanne," which always brings me to tears. But instead the musical order was switched, and I was blindsided by the beautiful song "Fire and Rain" by James Taylor, which starts out with her name, Suzanne, and has significant lyrics about wanting to see her again. I had goose bumps throughout the entire song and I happily knew that she was checking in.

Since Spirit is energy and electricity, it is likely that stormy weather makes communication with Spirit easier. The positive ions and lightning that occur during a storm provide a perfect setting for Spirit to make contact. Watch for postcards the next time your weather turns a bit wild.

Finding Symbolic Items

Suzanne loved anything that sparkled: rhinestones, sequins, gemstones, and crystal light catchers, as well as polished rocks and crystals. As a child she never wore girly things, but as a classical dancer during her first stage performance, her dance master told her she needed to wear ear studs that would catch the light. That did it. She was a convert to all things that caught the light and reflected color. In her twenties, she began wearing silver-beaded bracelets and hardly ever took them off. Silver necklaces too, with beads and stones, and for a while in her Gothic period, a silver ring in her nose. In her last years, as her lungs became weaker and she became increasingly housebound, she took to buying semiprecious gems as a hobby. They didn't cost much and it made her so happy to find these lovely things in the mail to light up her day. She often made jewelry out of them to add to her collection of necklaces and earrings. So imagine my surprise when I found a gift that could have only come from her.

We had a house for many years in the Hamptons, and Suzanne liked to visit to walk on the beach, swim in the pool, check out the stars, and enjoy our birds and wildlife. I had an herb garden on one side of the property with gravel walkways between the herbal beds. This was not her favorite haunt. However, as she liked rocks and crystals, she once said that someday I should really investigate the small pellets of gravel that made up the walkways—there might be something interesting in them to polish and keep.

After Suzanne died, one summer afternoon I thought about those words as I was weeding the gravel in the herb garden. I saw the sun shining on something metal in the small rocks near me. It was a tiny silver bead, and then another, and another, until I had a handful of tiny silver beads exactly like the ones she always wore. And then I saw a glimmer of iridescent blue in the pebbles. I picked up a tiny gemstone hidden among the gray stones. This was another small, mystical moment, causing my heart to soar and to be thankful for her messages. I have all of those silver beads now in a special box on my desk. I look at them and when I am at a low point, moving the beads through my hands helps to heal me and cheer me up.

Mike and I were on our way to meet up with family to watch our then fourteen-year-old granddaughter, Stephanie, play soccer in a tournament in Las Vegas. We would be there for a week. Stephanie and Suzanne had lots of love between them and a special sort of bond, so I felt my youngest daughter was going to be near on this trip. Mike had never been to Las Vegas and I had not visited since I was in my early twenties. I thought it might be quite an adventure.

Suzanne was heavy on my mind during the flight. Soon we would be with my family: Jennifer; son-in-law, Mark; and grandkids, Kevin and Stephanie. In a bittersweet moment I thought that if only Suzanne were here, my family would be complete. Just then, Mike reached into his airplane seat pocket for a magazine when he spied it. "Look at this! A penny!" he exclaimed, reminding me that a penny is our talisman, a postcard from her. "She's here." Her postcard-confirmed it. She was with us. I started to relax into the flight and anticipated family time—Spirit and all.

As I've mentioned, the number twenty-three was very significant to Suzanne. After showing me a tattoo she'd had done on her wrist when she was living in San Francisco, I yelled at her, "Why would you do that?" I was not a fan of body art at the time. She explained to me that she loved the mystical connotations of the prime number—the theory that all happenings can be connected in the Law of Five. Twenty-three is made up of the numbers two for balance and three for creativity. These two things she sought all of her life.

Mike and I drove our rental car to the Las Vegas outdoor soccer complex, located the field that Stephanie would be playing on, and walked over to the rest of the family just as the game was starting. We located Stephanie on the playing field by her bouncing ponytail and sweet face. Then I noticed she was wearing the number twenty-three. My daughter, Jennifer, turned to us and after hugs all around I realized that she had on a necklace with a soccer icon and the number twenty-three too. I thought Suzanne was letting us know that magic was there. If I was a person who gambled, I would have played the number twenty-three!

I suppose if I were not open to or aware of Suzanne, I could have not have noticed or would perhaps even have dismissed these postcard messages, but I am so happy I saw and felt them all. They continue to come to both Mike and me to this day and bring a smile and a metaphysical hug when one is needed.

Receiving an unexpected message or what I call a postcard from a loved one is an unexpected joy. This joy creates a moment of stillness in your mind wherein you are able to transcend the everyday. Time stops, the veil lifts, and you feel truly and completely alive and connected to all that is.

Every time it rains
It rains pennies from heaven
Don't you know each cloud contains
Pennies from heaven

"PENNIES FROM HEAVEN"
BY ARTHUR JOHNSTON AND
JOHNNY BURKE

A Penny for Her Thoughts

What joy it is to find a postcard in unexpected forms and places! But first you have to look and be mindful.

My mother loved to walk, and when I was growing up we lived in a place where walking to stores and friends was easy to do. I often went with her. But when I was a little girl, a long walk seemed a bit arduous and boring to me. She suggested I be observant to the things around me while I walked, because—who knew?—I might find something interesting on the way: a beautiful bird, a wildflower, some treasure, even a coin or two on the sidewalk. Walking became fun! I repeated this advice to my girls as they were growing up, and it became a game for us as well. Look around—what can you see?

After Suzanne died, for some reason I started to see pennies everywhere. Each time I have found them, she has been present in my thoughts. I have found them in the oddest places. I have found them in my own city, on trips, in foreign countries, even in my dreams. Each time I find one, it is a reiteration of "I am here."

One morning shortly after her death, I opened the door of my apartment to pick up the newspaper waiting for me when I saw a penny right there on the floor. The sight of it gave me chills and a sense of profound joy. "So, what is this about?" I wondered. Was this from Suzanne? I thought it might be but I wanted some other confirmation. I got the confirmation when I spoke to the medium Nell again.

More from Nell and Suzanne

I happened to be in San Francisco for the funeral of Sheila, the sweet mother of Jenn, one of Suzanne's best friends. On a hopeful whim I gave Nell a call the night before I left for home, hoping I could reach her in the right time zone to see what else she and Suzanne would tell me. I am glad I did because Nell told me some wonderful things. Nell said again that Suzanne was a very strong Spirit and was in a happy place now and out of pain.

Then Suzanne told Nell to tell me she would always be with me and when I saw an unexpected penny, it was she directing me and/or Mike to it. It was a postcard to us, and she would leave many postcard messages of one sort or another, not just pennies, in the future. She said I had to remain open, aware, and remember coincidences do not happen. You have read this to be true in the previous chapter, "Interesting Things"! Again, among lots of other information she said she loved me very much and that I had to get busy and live the rest of my life. Nell said to call her again so we could talk some more. I planned to do just that.

The Pennies Begin

The next morning, I left for the San Francisco airport to go home to New York. I was deep in thought about my daughter the entire ride, contemplating the meaning of my talk with Nell. The taxi pulled up to the departure area. I opened the door and put out my foot, almost stepping on a shiny penny. Suzanne! I picked it up and put it in my pocket. Pondering this while in the security line, I looked down to find yet another penny near my feet! I had goose bumps and such a rush of emotion it was hard not to cry out in the crowded line. Now I had two pennies in my pocket to hold on to during the long trip and keep my daughter near.

The long trip home was thankfully uneventful. To relieve muscle tension on flights, I often stretch my legs by walking up and down the aisles, so I always book an aisle seat. After landing, I stood and began to walk down the aisle to the exit. I looked down to see yet one more penny shining there on the carpet. What? My heart leaped out of my chest with joy. I had not spotted that one on my frequent walks. *Do you get it, Mom? I am here.* Now it was established that those pennies are postcards from Suzanne.

Both Mike and I have found our pennies when she is on our mind. Sometimes we have been missing her, talking about her, wishing she were here for support during a difficult time, or remembering her with joy and happiness and laughter. We miss her at holidays and we miss her when we would normally ask her advice on decisions, and we miss her when we travel because we want to share those times with her too.

Pennies are a way of letting me know she is here. You may have other forms of a talisman, or, as I call it, a postcard from your loved one. Figure out a common object, song, color, or animal that has meaning for you both. Be aware when they appear. Coincidences do not happen.

The following stories and occurrences are just a few of the many postcards in penny form we have received from our Suzanne.

Church Offering

One Sunday in church shortly after her death, I was really missing my daughter and I was more than a little weepy. Something the rector said about love rang true. I was finding it hard to keep the tears from rolling down my cheeks. At this moment I heard Suzanne say to me very clearly, "Mom, don't dwell in the past. You have to go forward into a new mental place." Drying my eyes, I thought, *Okay, for Suzanne I will try again.*

After the service, Mike and I stopped at our local supermarket for a few things. Still upset, my eye caught sight of something moving on the floor. It was a shiny penny rolling toward my feet where it stopped right in front of me. We laughed about that and then Mike said, "Look!" Another penny was peeking out on the floor a few feet away. Our hearts were lifted—we sailed home hand in hand. It was a good reminder to be happy and that she is near.

Bridle Trail Mystery

Early one spring morning, I was reading in the *New York Times* about caretakers of dying loved ones insisting that the dying continue to eat and drink even though they have no interest in food. All they want to do is to die quietly and peacefully. I thought of Suzanne then. Toward the end of her life, she suffered from appetite loss and told me, "Mom, there just isn't any food invented on Earth that tastes good now." Remembering her words was painful.

I was in an awful mood, unable to shake my sadness, griping at Mike and swallowing back tears and anger. That afternoon, to cheer ourselves up, we took our favorite walk in Central Park on the sandy Bridle Path once used for saddle horses and then up the trail to the wild, bird-filled Ramble. A walk in nature is often just the thing needed for me to calm my mind. As we were still talking and thinking about Suzanne, she came into my head and told me, "Don't be so sad. I am fine now and happier than ever. Please stop thinking about the small time in my life that I suffered. Think of all the happy times we had together. My death does not define me."

I looked down then and spied a small but familiar shine. I bent down and picked up a penny half buried in the sandy ground. I have never before found a penny on the Central Park Bridle Path—it is a very unlikely spot for a penny to be. It is a path we have walked a thousand times before. These are the moments that keep us both realizing that she is with us still. She is letting us know she's happy and wants us to be happy too.

Don't Cry, Mom

Some time ago, I was shopping in a home store that was a favorite of Suzanne's. She was such a window-shopper and investigator of new things, particularly, as noted earlier, if those things had a sparkle of some kind. I was silently talking to her under my breath as I went through the store, wishing so much she was with me, remembering how we had laughed at the outrageous things people market and customers actually buy. Then I noticed a display of kitchen sponges that were made of a bright pink-orange, neon sparkly metallic and, laughing out loud, I turned to show her.

Then the tears came. I could not help them—my heart had such an empty feeling. I said, "Suzanne, why aren't you with me here today?" and tried to pull myself together as other shoppers passed by. I then heard her say very clearly, "Mom, I am always here with you." *Okay, good*, I thought. Taking a deep breath, I felt her presence next to me.

I bought my items and began to walk to the front door of the store. Setting my packages down to put on my coat, I saw it. On the floor at my feet near one of my packages was my talisman, my postcard, the penny that always brings a smile to my face and joy to my heart!

Butterfly Kiss

Mike and I often go to the Metropolitan Opera House in New York. Suzanne enjoyed opera too and had accompanied us there a few times. One evening not long after she'd transitioned, Mike and I had tickets for *Madama Butterfly*. My energy was so very low from grieving that it was all I could do to get dressed and go. I had some worries about seeing this tragic opera where the sweet Japanese woman is deserted by her American husband and separated from her child, and in the end commits suicide. I was afraid of the memories this would unlock.

Lately I had been studying Spanish, so I switched the translator at the back of the seat in front of me from the English language to Spanish. I entertained myself by trying to decipher the words while listening to the beautiful voices and music of Puccini.

But then I made the mistake of looking back at the stage during the third act, when Butterfly is waiting for her husband to appear to take her child. It was very bad timing on my part. The grief of losing a child hit me then and I started to crumble. Tears started running down my cheeks and I knew in a few seconds that large wails would start to escape me and all would be lost there in the Grand Tier of the Metropolitan Opera House. I silently screamed for Suzanne to help me. "Quickly come and aid my agony," I said, "or your mom will have to leave her seat before the last act, and everyone will stare and wonder what is wrong with this woman." She came then, with a cool breeze on my face and a kiss on my cheek. I instantly took a deep breath and became calm. I blessed her for this timely rescue and she left.

At the end of the performance Mike and I slowly gathered our things and got up to leave. I heard something drop. Looking down, we saw that a nickel had landed on the floor in front of us. As Mike picked it up and gave it to me, I thought, *Okay, this one was good for a nickel.* I left with joy in my heart and dry eyes.

Not Too Far, Please

Chris is a wonderful medium. You will read more about him in the chapter "Mediums for Healing," which details people who have this special gift. One year he did a reading for us the day after Suzanne's birthday. In the reading, Suzanne said she was going to be busy and not around quite as much, but if I needed her and called her, she would come. I thought I was ready to handle it.

Nope.

Boy, did I sense she was gone. I could not feel her almost constant presence or hear her voice in my head. I saw no uncommon lights, felt no brushes of hands, heard no odd sounds, and found no pennies. I fell into an awful depression and actually got very sick. I feared she would not come back and I would have to finish this life without her Spirit near me. This carried on for a few weeks until I couldn't stand it any longer and I screamed for her. One evening I ranted and cried, and then quite suddenly all was well as I felt her presence fill me.

The next day, I found a penny again on the street. I began our conversations and was soothed. I'm not sure if this was a test to see if I could handle Suzanne being gone or to see if I could have some assurance that if she went away for a while, she would come back if I went a little crazy. So now we know. I am stronger and more comfortable in the knowledge my daughter will hear me if I am distressed. *Whew.* If I yell for help, help will come.

For Mike's Heart

A few years after Suzanne's death Mike was diagnosed with atrial fibrillation. This fluctuation of the heart rhythm is not uncommon after a major surgery like the one he had for diverticulitis. The simplest fix is to try a cardiac reversion using an electric shock to the heart. That procedure, although seemingly noninvasive and simple, actually stops and restarts the heart, which was not a comforting prospect.

For this to happen, Mike had to be an outpatient at a hospital and he would be there all day. It was the same hospital where previously both Suzanne and Mike had almost died. It scared me going back there even for an outpatient procedure. My skin crawled just walking past it. Before we left for the hospital, I asked Suzanne to come with us. Getting into the cab, I thought it would be really great to find a penny. But looking around the cab, I found none. So we got out and began our long walk a half a block down the sidewalk to the hospital entrance. *Now would be a really good time for one of those pennies, Suzanne*, I continued to think nervously. Ah! Looking down, I spotted it. At the side of the street, almost at the entrance, was a penny half buried in the grass. We grinned and I put it in Mike's coat pocket.

Of course, she was with us on this most difficult day, giving us support.

A Hug

Mike and I went out looking for a comfy chair to replace a worn one in our den. We went to a part of the city that Suzanne and I had frequented. There was a familiar Starbucks on the corner, an art store across the street, and a favorite clothing store next to it. Being in this neighborhood brought back so many memories. I mentioned to Mike this was a trigger spot for me. He hugged me and we went into the furniture store. He immediately walked over to an audio display and sat down to rest in one of the two chairs there, testing it out for comfort. I started to sit in the other one and then I pointed to Mike, unable to speak. A penny was right in the middle of the seat, waiting for me to see it! Finding that shining penny felt like a warm and wonderful hug. More important, it also served to remove the trigger reaction from this part of town. Now I remember the reassuring hug of the penny instead of grief when I find myself in that part of the city.

Mother's Day

Mother's Day has not been an easy day for me and is hard for all mothers who have lost a child and for all children who have lost a mother. The media frenzy leading up to it is not helpful for a grieving heart full of memories. With Suzanne in Spirit and Jennifer three thousand miles away in California, I am alone with my thoughts of them both. While she was alive, Suzanne was always so sweet on Mother's Day, often gifting me with a beautiful handwritten card she'd crafted, expressing her love for me. Small bouquets were left at my front door for me to find.

Now on Mother's Day, Mike and I often go the Metropolitan Museum to enjoy the art and have a nice lunch. The Met is a place where I can get lost in the beautiful art and objects of our human history. Art museums have played a large part in my life with my daughters, so I connect with them there.

On this particular Mother's Day, the weather was soft and dry. New green leaves were budding and birds were busy. It was a perfect spring day and I felt Suzanne with us. On the way to the bus after our museum visit, Mike yelled "Stop!" He bent down, and on the crowded sidewalk was a penny waiting for us. She was and is still gifting me.

Christmas Eve

The holidays are always a hard time for those who grieve. In the early years after Suzanne's passing, I just wanted to hide my head and never leave home until the weeks of forced holiday cheer were over. To make it doubly hard, her passing had been on January 28, just a month after Christmas.

On our way home after having dinner with good friends on Christmas Eve, I felt the pain in my heart beginning to kick up. Mike and I arrived at our building in a taxi near midnight and I tried to gather my emotions before the cab door was opened by our building's doorman. It was a rainy, dark moonless night and bitter cold. Stepping out of the cab first, Mike suddenly bent down and picked something up from the street. He rose, smiled at me, and put that something into my hand. It was a most welcome penny. At once the night was not so dark, illuminated as it was by the glow of the penny. I am reminded in my darkest days and nights that my daughter is with me and there is no need for grief.

The Neighbors

On one of Suzanne's birthdays I found myself again with swollen eyes and a heavy heart. This was before we combined our apartments, so her place still had a separate entrance. I went through her door and into the kitchen to pour myself her favorite drink: Jack Daniels and Coke. It tasted pretty good and I felt better as I lifted a toast to my daughter. I then went out to pick up flowers and cupcakes for our evening birthday celebration. After coming home, I started to go into her place to water houseplants and just sit in quiet remembrance for a while in that *Thin Place* where Spirit contact is easy. (Decribed in a previous chapter, The Long Road Traveled, *Finding Grace*) Just as I was about to open the door, I spied something bright and shiny on the neighbor's doorstep. Her penny. I figured it was Suzanne's kind of joke, and I added it to the pile while thinking of her ability to lift my spirits at just the right time with a penny postcard.

A Playful Plethora of Pennies

Mike loves to sail with his buddy Dennis. One morning after he had left the apartment for the boat, I was feeling a bit lonely. I mentally asked for a postcard from Suzanne. Cleaning the top of the bureau in the bedroom, I scooped some small change into my hand, but something escaped onto the floor and hit the baseboard. A penny. An instant grin appeared on my face.

I had lots of places to go to in the city that morning, so while walking down the sidewalk, I had hoped to find another postcard. I heard her say, "But I already sent you a penny today." Ah, yes," I said, "but maybe more will turn up." I thought about how much she had loved shopping at the store I was in. When I put out my hand for change and saw it was four pennies, I giggled out loud and felt her vibration run through me.

I had to cross the street for a final errand. After placing a handful of pennies in my hand for change, the cashier apologized, saying, "I am so sorry for giving you all these pennies, but pennies are all I have at the moment."

What? I thought to myself as I heard her say, "Okay, Mom, is that enough now?" I do believe I laughed out loud all the way home.

Lost but Found

Mike and I traveled with some friends to beautiful Durango, Colorado, to spend some time in nature and hike the mountain trails there. Although I had been thinking about how much Suzanne would like this scenery, I held no hope that I would find a penny in the wilderness. One trail we hiked was littered with huge twelve-foot-high boulders from some ancient quake activity. Somehow we took a wrong turn and for a minute lost our way. As we all stood together, trying to figure out which way to go, my gaze fell upon the tall boulder we were leaning against. Looking at it closely, I could see at eye level a natural crack that circled the middle of it. This crack was stuffed with hundreds of pennies! Lost on a mountain trail in the middle of nowhere, we find pennies! In a rock! My jaw dropped, my mind stopped, and I was filled with her vibration.

All I could do was point to them while Mike took pictures. Suzanne led us to that boulder as if saying to me with humor, "What? You want a penny? Here's a few!"

Ashes

For a few years, Suzanne's ashes remained in the black box they'd come home in and sat on a shelf in my clothing closet where I saw them every day. I was strangely comforted by them. Over time, I thought perhaps she would like her ashes to be in something prettier and be out in the open instead of in a closet. I finally found a large Chinese urn I thought would be very nice in the living room. I was unsure if she would like it since she was not too crazy about Chinese decor. I was talking to Mike about my indecision as I unwrapped the vase from its packing material. I went to throw away the wrapping in the room off the common hallway where we deposited recycling, and as I came back, I passed the hallway bench near our door. A penny was sitting right in the middle of the bench! Apparently, she approved of the urn.

Question answered.

Pennies for Friends

Suzanne's postcards pennies have even shown up for friends, including my friend Barbara.

I have known Barbara for most of my adult life. She has been a good friend and was a sometime sitter for me when the girls were young and we all lived in California. Barbara moved east to marry Craig, but we stayed in touch. With me still in California, Barbara and Craig took Suzanne under their wing when Suzanne went to New York City to dance in the Joffrey Ballet's summer program. Barbara knew of Suzanne's pennies and how she moved my pictures and fooled with my clocks. One morning she had to tell me the following tale.

Barbara needed to bring breakfast rolls to a client on her way to work, so stopped at a bakery that was across the street from a popular craft store. Suzanne had often shopped in that craft store for art supplies and creative ideas. She could spend hours going over all the merchandise.

Looking at the store sign, Barbara was thinking about Suzanne and her artwork when she opened the car door. As she started to step down, she spied, lying on the ground, a shiny penny at her feet. Taking in a sharp breath, she said, "Suzanne!" Barbara felt her presence then and she loved the good vibes it gave her.

When she arrived home and told Craig the story, he replied, "Of course, it was Suzanne. Look at her artwork hanging on the wall in the den; the pictures are all askew!"

Not Everyone

Not everyone is open to Spirit and this is a personal choice and not a judgment. We all need to travel through our lives in our own way with our own beliefs, with eyes and hearts open to what makes sense to us individually. I have the utmost respect for the alternate paths that others travel.

We have old and dear friends who live out of state. They had a son die tragically young many years ago and then lost a second son to cancer. We have shared many moments in our long friendship, but this common experience of a death of a child is not something anyone would want to share.

These friends have known my children for a long time. It is hard for them when I talk of the connection I still have with Suzanne. I would love for them to be able to perhaps think about the idea that their sons are really still nearby and able to help ease the pain of their loss. I had told them a few times the stories of the pennies and other phenomona so perhaps they might be open to finding a postcard from their sons.

Then, during a visit they made to New York City, we all attended an art show at the Guggenheim Museum. It featured the unique art of James Turrell. Turrell works in the mysteries of neon light and color. I thought this was an installation that Suzanne would love also.

The entire museum's first floor had been transformed into a space of changing colors emanating from the tall ceiling but filling the very air of the entire floor. People were invited to sit or lie down on mats to more easily experience the feeling of light and color affecting mood and place. They were beautiful chakra colors fading into one another: red, orange, yellow, green, blue, violet, and white. Over and over again the colors of the light kept changing. Entranced, we lay on the mats and let the colors and emotions they brought up wash through us.

I thought how much Suzanne would have loved this experience and felt she was with us. As I got up from the mat, I saw a shiny penny lying right at my head and felt incredible exhilaration and joy. After pointing it out to Mike, we grinned and said to each other that, yes, of course she was here. I showed it to our friends but I didn't receive much of a response, so I said nothing more.

A few days later at home on the sofa sharing a pot of tea, my friend and I talked about the deaths of our children. My friend said in some ways she was a little envious of my continuing connection with Suzanne even though she could not bring herself to believe in the afterlife. I again told her she could have a connection with her sons too, and that she should just be open to the messages. When our guests were ready for the trip to the airport to go home, our doorman was ready to hail the cab.

A cab pulled to the front of the building and as they began to walk toward it, our doorman noticed a penny lying right by the cab door on the street. He said, "This is your lucky day—look what I found." Appearing caught off guard but saying nothing, our friends waited for the door to be opened to enter the back seat. After opening the door, our doorman said, "Look, here is another one for you," as yet another penny was waiting on the floor of the cab. Again, no response.

These encounters with our friends pointed out to us that not everyone will wish to, or try to, see or hear messages from other side of the veil. Most important, this is perfectly okay. In these cases it's best to let the conversation go.

Travel Gifts

What has truly amazed me is the finding of a penny while traveling out of the country. I certainly had no expectations of the bliss I would experience when finding Suzanne's postcard outside the United States. You can't imagine my surprise to find pennies in other countries. The message is to always be open and aware of your postcards, no matter where you might be

Lounging Around

To take a warm break from one cold and snowy eastern winter, Mike and I spent a relaxing week in Puerto Rico at a beach resort. Each day we both took two towels and plunked them on lounge chairs near the sand, and read, napped, or walked as far as we could down the beach. One afternoon, memories were heavy on my mind as I remembered how much Suzanne had enjoyed walking on the beach with me all of her life.

With those memories of her as a girl skipping along beside me, Mike and I left our books behind and set out for a nice long stroll, with the warm water tickling our toes. Returning to our lounge chairs, I thought to rearrange my towels neatly. I picked up one and there sitting prettily on the second towel was a shiny penny. It was not there before and now it was. How, I do not know. There she was, enjoying yet another beach walk.

Italian Euro Penny

While visiting Amalfi, Italy, we went into the lovely cathedral there. It is a beautiful building set at the top of many stairs and has a lovely cloister with a tended garden. In the church Mike said we should light a candle for Suzanne. I lit mine, asking for understanding of this life-and-death thing. Unbeknownst to me at the time, Mike asked Suzanne to somehow give me a penny. We came out of the cathedral, walked down the stairs, and turned at the bottom to go toward the Paper Museum. My eyes turned toward the uneven ground to guide my step. Then I spotted a shiny thing lying between the stones. It was a euro penny! What a wonderful and unbelievable gift!

She is with us wherever we go.

German Euro Penny

One summer we took a vacation, first to the Swiss Alps, then down the Rhine River on a boat tour. We stopped at some lovely ancient towns along the way on the tour. In Germany one of the towns was called Rüdesheim. This town still has some lovely medieval structures, which surprisingly had been left standing after the two world wars had taken down so many ancient buildings.

Walking toward the center of town, we found ourselves on a narrow cobblestone street. I looked up at the street name. It was Keller, her grandmother's family name. "Suzanne," I said. "Look at that!" Mike and I poked in quaint craft stores and I said to Suzanne, "Where are you? You would love this pretty town. It could have some family history. I really miss you." Mike wanted a coffee, so we went to sit at one of the open tables at a little sidewalk café and ordered. Something caught my eye. There at my feet was a shiny euro penny. There was my answer! She liked the town too and somehow directed us to the table with the euro penny on the ground.

Mont-Saint-Michel, France

Mont-Saint-Michel is an ancient tidal island fortress in Normandy on the upper coast of France. I have wanted to see this truly magical place since reading about it as a young girl. After discovering it in books, my girls also wished to see it someday. Finally, Mike and I had a chance to see and explore that beautiful structure. Once only accessible when the tide was out, the immense Gothic building served many masters, including Benedictine monks and royalty. It also served as a prison in the reign of Louis XI. It is now a UNESCO site.

When it was a prison, the bodies of executed prisoners were thrown into a deep pit until they were removed from the island when and if the time and tide was right. On the tour, one of the stops was the pit. Oh, no, not old bones! I declined to look into the pit, thinking I would rather see just about anything other than a place where so many bodies once lay and still might. I began to quickly walk away. I heard Suzanne: "Mom, go back and look at the pit. It isn't what you think it is. Really, you will like it." Listening to her against my better judgment, I did turn around and slowly edge up to the pit, peering in with trepidation. To my surprise I found it filled with shiny change from pilgrims and tourists who had visited. On the top, among all the other coins, staring at me was a shining penny.

I must listen to my daughter when she speaks to me. She does not give me bad advice!

Even Saigon

We arrived in Saigon very tired as it was the end of a long trip through Southeast Asia with good friends. This was to be our last few days before heading home. Our friends Walter and Linda had never known Suzanne but have always been interested in our journey with her. She was often part of our conversations. Upon arriving at our hotel, Mike and I decided to go straight to our room, rest up, and meet Walter and Linda later for dinner. We walked into our room and waited for our luggage to arrive. Exhausted, I started to lie on the bed when I saw it. A penny right in the middle of the king-size bed! I looked and shook my head a few times before I really believed a U.S. penny was there, waiting for us in our Saigon hotel room. Apparently, Suzanne had been listening!

Pandemic Pennies

As I finished this book, the world changed. The highly contagious corona virus called COVID-19 came upon the world at the end of 2019. First in China and then Europe, it hit the United States with full force in early 2020.

New York City was the center of the pandemic in the United States. In the Spring of 2020 more than 20,000 people died in the city alone, with over 200,000 infected and ill. Our hospitals were overrun with the sick and dying, and our health care personnel worked without sufficient equipment or relief. Essential city workers were heroes too. Many of them became fallen heroes as illness overtook those who could not isolate themselves. They worked hard instead of staying home, trying to keep the city running during a lockdown.

As the city masked up, kept a social distance of at least six feet, and we learned again how to wash our hands, the infection rate in the city slowly receded. Then COVID-19 slowly continued to spread across the country.

Measures were put in place to try to contain the outbreak. In New York, schools and businesses closed. All travel stopped. Other countries gathered their own and closed their doors. The entire globe became quiet. In the cities the sound of sirens and birdsong became the norm.

We became a cashless society. Afraid to touch money or another's hand, those who could paid for everything by credit card or ordered online. Since very little currency was being used, less change was in circulation. Banks were even asking for rolled change to be turned in. I lost hope of finding Suzanne's pennies. How could it happen? The city was a ghost town.

We found pennies anyway! As we walked on our empty streets, she would suddenly come to mind and there would be a penny right in front of us. Although she was always seemingly nearby with her usual methods of picture-moving, loud bangs, heavy presence, light displays, and clear dreams, her pennies now took on a deeper delight. She put a much needed smile on our masked faces and joy in our hearts. We found pennies in the middle of the street, on the sidewalks, and on buses. They were happy pennies during a time of deep sorrow. "All is okay—I am here, Mom," they seemed to say.

On and On

My postcard pennies continue be found. Those I have described are just some of the wonderful instances of her messages. Since Suzanne has promised to always be with me, I fully expect the pennies and other forms of postcards to be found until we are together again. If you are open to the possibilities of the universe, you can find your own special talisman and be soothed and delighted by messages too.

Finding a talisman or postcard from a loved one is such a unique moment. The absolute joy it brings is indescribable. Normal time and existence stop. You are momentarily lifted from this world into theirs. For that moment, life is richer, fuller, and more colorful, and you are filled with an unearthly wonder and love. You cannot help but smile, and with an unexplainable lightness of being you leave your grief behind and reenter the world with a better understanding of the connectedness of all things.

We are such stuff as dreams are made on,
And our little life is rounded with a sleep.

THE TEMPEST

BY WILLIAM SHAKESPEARE

Dreams

So much has been said about our dreams and what they might mean. Large numbers of books have been written about them, and philosophers and psychiatrists have tried to understand their meanings and the purpose of our dream state. But no one really knows what happens when we dream.

From a spiritual standpoint, I feel our dreams are a way our loved ones can visit with us for a while in an easy and relaxed way. Certainly not every dream involves Spirit, but do not discount the wonderful dreams you may have or may have had of departed family or loved ones, even pets who come to visit with you. Waking up happier for no known reason can be the result of a visit in a dream you do not remember. Mediums have said to me if the remembering will cause you more grief from waking and feeling the loss, then it is better to leave the details of the dream unrecalled.

Suzanne has come to both Mike and me repeatedly in our dreams. We wake up with smiles and happiness that we were able to spend time together. The dreams are another way for her to converse with us and make us think outside the box. They are always insightful and leave us with joy and oftentimes in absolute awe.

Keeping a Dream Diary

I often rue the fact sometimes my dreams, although often vivid upon waking, fade so quickly as I come into my fully conscious mind and start to think about the tasks of the day. If you have trouble remembering your dreams, you might consider keeping a small notepad and a pen next to your bed so you can quickly jot down what you remember upon waking. Even a few buzz words will lead your mind back into your dream world long enough for you to enjoy the visit. Over time, you can train your mind to remember your dreams for a longer period.

The following are just some of the memorable dreams that Mike and I have had with Suzanne. Nights can be real adventures. Sometimes she is with me in my dreams and sometimes with Mike, and even more interesting are the times when we are all together in the same dream.

The Gift

One evening soon after her death, I went to bed horribly sad, wishing so much that things were different. As I began to drift off, I heard Suzanne clearly saying to me, "Mom, do not use your pain as a shield," telling me to move forward and to let others help me with my grief instead of backing away from it. Then a beautiful, shimmering woman I recognized as my daughter was in front of me, holding something toward me in her hands. It was a box that opened to reveal a clear ball of changing colors. She said, "This is a gift. It will help you move from realm to realm." I took the ball and she said, "A ball can reveal all of its sides whereas a box will always have a side away from sight." I woke, feeling extremely light and happy while thinking about those words and what they meant.

A few nights later, again I dreamed of her. This time she said, "There are no sharp edges in nature. Everything is rounded, and so it is in this realm." She also reiterated, "Remember you have been given a gift. Now you can live free from anxiety about me. Live it, evolve, you have time." I am trying to heed these thought-provoking words.

My attempts at art are so much better now that I start with rounded edges. I am trying to round all of my sharp edges, mentally, socially, and emotionally. I do realize my sharp edges have been my shield and my emotional protection. This is a hard habit to change, to let others in and not to respond to perceived threats so thoughtlessly.

New Clothes

Suzanne asks us to grow and evolve in subtle ways in dreams too. When we were traveling in Naples, Italy, Mike had a wonderful dream. In it he felt he needed a new suit of clothes. Suzanne appeared to him and said, "Mike, try on these clothes!" and handed him a bundle. He tried them on but said to her, "These just don't feel right yet," and gave them back. Ha! At least he was trying them on and she was showing them to him. If it hadn't been Suzanne urging him to do it, he would never have even tried them on. A change of clothes often means a change in thinking.

Uplifting Moments

Suzanne could be quite physical as well.

I was thinking about Suzanne one evening before going to sleep and how much I truly missed her physical hugs. I had not been feeling well at all and really needed one of those healing hugs. When I was almost but not quite asleep, her energy came to me and electrified my body so much that I was shaking and smiling. Then she moved my body by lifting me up a few inches off the bed and moving me from the edge closer to the center. Goose bumps galore!

I have not felt so much love and electrical energy ever. I thought she was becoming so much stronger. I laughed and smiled and was so comforted. I slowly came back into full consciousness but the experience had been so real, my heart was just pounding in my chest. I thanked her profusely for that amazing and healing visit.

And Funny Too

In life Suzanne had a terrific sense of humor. She could be silly, very ironic, even slapstick. It seems that had not changed! I remember on one occasion Mike and I had been irritable and cranky. Going to bed unhappy, I dreamed that Mike and I were standing together, and all of a sudden she appeared between us. She had a mustache and a short Fu Manchu beard. I asked, "What are you doing wearing a beard?" And she chuckled and replied, "I wanted to make you both lighten up and laugh!" She then removed it. She did make us laugh, just as she always had. Funny girl.

Mike reported one morning, with awe in his voice, that Suzanne had invaded his dream. He was dreaming in Technicolor and she popped in, wearing all black (no news there), and all the color left his dream. He said,

"Hey, why are you in the middle of my dream?" She was sitting down and looking up at him above her black small-rimmed glasses like she often did. Not saying anything, she got up, smiled, did her very unique funky chicken Suzanne dance, and left.

Not to be outdone, I discovered the next night she came into my dream. She popped in and said, "Look, Mom," and pointed to the floor. Yes, there were two shiny pennies there. Now I find them in my dreams too.

In Times of Stress

Suzanne often comes to us in a dream when we have heavy worries, physical or mental. I think she does this in order to let us know that, whatever happens, she is not far.

Mike had been experiencing some unusual pressure in his chest, which seemed to have started after his ablation procedure for atrial fibrillation. His cardiac surgeon did not seem concerned, and his EKGs were normal. But the problem persisted and increased in degree of pain and occurrence. This was very troubling. Then one evening, in a semidream state, Mike saw Suzanne appearing in our bedroom. She was wearing a diaphanous white gown and moved to sit in the chair at the corner of the room. She sat quietly while we both gathered around her, so glad to see her. She said nothing but just kept smiling at Mike until she faded away. He came to consciousness with a grin and in peace.

A few days later, we saw our regular cardiologist who confirmed it was no doubt a muscle issue and would heal itself. Of course, later that day at the paint store when we were waiting for our paint and chatting about the dream, we found a shiny penny just for good measure.

Connections

Sometimes I find that the dreams are about connections to be made on the other plane or reassurances of the connections we have there.

Brenda is one such connection. She was my lifelong friend whom I had met in childhood. She was also very close to my daughters often stepping in as a treasured Aunt. Brenda studied ballet as a girl and danced in the San Francisco Ballet until an injury ended that career. She was the inspiration for Suzanne to dance. Brenda became an accomplished actress in Hollywood. She tragically lost her only child when he was just six and never adjusted to the horrible grief of losing a child. Unable to cope, she committed suicide a few years after losing him. Her death hit us all very hard. I would often dream of her visiting me and chatting like we normally did. I once asked her in a dream, "I thought you had died?" She answered me with a laugh, "No, silly, I didn't die, I just moved to another place. We can still visit like always." We had "flying" dreams where we would hold hands and take off to fly above the trees, or swing low down the streets and through valleys. Exhuberient, ex-hilarating fun. Therefore, it was no stretch to have her appear in a dream with Suzanne and I.

In one such dream, Suzanne and I were in a house that was all white and light. She was a grown woman. We were talking about our friend Brenda who had passed on thirty years prior and questioning where she might be now. Suzanne said she wanted to talk to Brenda. I told her it was hard for me to find her when she was working as she could be anywhere, but I would try my best.

Suddenly, the phone rang and Suzanne walked over to answer it. She was standing with her back to me but she just glowed. I could hear both of the conversations. The caller was a woman and I recognized Brenda's voice. Brenda asked who she was talking to, and Suzanne replied, "Where are you? We have been trying to find you!"

Brenda asked, "Who is this?" and Suzanne replied, "It's Suzanne and I am the bartender in this house." We all laughed, and Brenda gave her address and said they would get together soon. With wonderful feelings of love and togetherness I woke up, smiling. I kept grinning all day, thinking the two of them would soon be together.

Friends

Many of Suzanne's friends and mine have called to tell me they've had dreams of her—happy dreams of dancing and laughing.

Suzy has been in our lives since before Suzanne was born. Suzy told me of a dream she had shortly after Suzanne passed. "I dreamed of her in the form of an iridescent goldfish, seemingly flowing in beautiful light. Suzanne told me we needed to heal our differences because 'the only thing that matters here is love.'" Suzy and I had not spoken for a number of years after having had a silly falling-out. I regret that a small and insignificant argument caused such a rift between us for so long but was thankful that my daughter, even in the afterlife, wanted to make it right.

Because of this dream, Suzy and I restarted our friendship.

Be Ready

Visits from Spirit in dreams can be so very healing and enlightening. But even in the dream state, Spirit can have a hard time making contact if one is surrounded by the pain of grief. Crying yourself to sleep does not put you in a place where you are ready to receive messages. Try to enter sleep in a calm, relaxed way. Breathe deeply and concentrate on good thoughts and memories. Remember the love between you and let that love take you into the dream world where you can find healing, love, humor, and connection.

*There are more things in heaven
and earth, Horatio,
Than are dreamt of in
your philosophy.*

HAMLET

BY WILLIAM SHAKESPEARE

Mediums for Healing

In my life I have not only read about but have also experienced moments with people who are blessed with gifts outside the realm of traditional life. These are people who have the ability to connect with the future as a psychic and/or to communicate with the other realm of existence as a medium.

Since the start of recorded civilization, humanity has written about, sometimes honored, and often hounded people with these unique gifts. But mankind has always looked for guidance outside itself and the world it can see.

There is a difference between a person who is psychic and one who is a medium. Both gifts can be present in the same person but not always. A psychic is able to sense things in this life, the past, and the future, but a medium can connect to those who have passed on. Generally, a psychic can have the gift of communicating with the other realm but that is not always true. A medium is a conduit to Spirit. Sensitive, intuitive people receive communication in different ways—some through sound/speech, others through visions, and sometimes both.

These gifted people have been a tremendous help to me in my life because although you may feel your loved one's presence, it is very soothing to actually speak to someone who has a gift of direct communication with the other side. There may be some issues you want to see if you can resolve by intervening in this way, or some important words to be heard or said. We are often at such a loss after the death of a loved one, and if we just get a few questions answered or be sure Spirit is still around us, it helps us in our daily lives.

Since I felt so comforted after my first experience talking with Nell, I was open to speaking with more of these gifted people. So, besides sweet Nell, I have spoken with a couple of other sensitives. I found Suzanne continues to repeat to me the things I most need to hear. I can see her twirling in frustration about this!

I think I get it now.

Chris

It is because of our friend Denise that Mike and I became acquainted with Chris. Denise has a dental hygienist practice in New York City, and we think she is absolutely the best. She also has a deep interest in Spirit and the afterlife. Denise and Suzanne struck up a friendship of mutual respect and admiration here in the city some years before Suzanne's death. Denise knew how much Mike and I were adrift when Suzanne passed, and she kept mentioning a fellow she knew whose main purpose was to help others find peace from grief. One day Denise gave me Chris's number and said to call him. But I was afraid that Suzanne might not be able to be reached, that Chris and I would not be able to connect with her. Unsure, I put Chris's number on my desk and looked at it daily, waiting until I felt it was the right time.

After many months of indecision and a great deal of angst, I made a call to Chris and am forever grateful that I did. Chris's voice and demeanor immediately put me at ease. I felt such a deep connection to him, and what he was saying to me, that my burden of grief was already lighter. Suzanne came in immediately as a very strong Spirit and was adamant that I celebrate her life and not her demise from Earth. She clearly said, "Please remember I am more than my death—remember my life with joy and I can be with you. It is hard for me to be with you when you have so much grief."

Lesson learned. Since I wanted to be able to feel her presence more deeply, I began to explore ways out of my grief so that further contact would be easier.

I have since spoken with Chris many times during the ensuing years. He has often repeated to me, "Suzanne will always be with you. Keep aware of her postcards and the many ways she will let you know she is near." Mike and I have done so, and we have found great happiness in keeping our minds open and alert. Chris is a good friend to us all now, including Suzanne. He says that Suzanne has helped him in guiding others on the spiritual plane to him and therefore they both have been able to help others.

When I said during a reading that I missed her physical presence, Suzanne said to Chris, "Mom, you should think of me still in San Francisco because when I lived there, we didn't see each other much but we talked all the time. We talk now, just differently." Chris related that Suzanne is near me when I am doing something creative. She, being such an artistic soul, enjoys watching me and her other friends create art and beauty. I always feel she is near me when I bring in and arrange fresh flowers or sit and work on my art, or open my mind to some new creative project. She said, "The creative mind is an open mind and I can come and be with you then." Creating beauty somehow allows a universal flow of feeling and love.

More from Nell

I talked to Nell again the November that Mike was in the hospital, very ill. I was frantic that he was sick and I was still feeling a lot of grief from Suzanne's death. I really needed to hear from my daughter, so I called Nell. Nell immediately responded. She said that my daughter was a strong Spirit and she was becoming a leader where she was. She said she had very big energy and she would continue to be my guide. Through Nell, Suzanne counseled me, telling me, "Regrets are not useful, so no more 'if only I had done thus and so.' You must keep writing because it's calming for you and the words you are writing are important. You must continue to draw and paint as well." My daughter reassured me that she was always there and for me, and that I should try to be happy. She said through Nell, "You know, Mom, you are a powerful and influential person, and you should own up to it and not shy away from your power." Suzanne went on, "The holidays are coming and try not to be upset by them because the holidays are really just a time for all people to express love."

I felt so much stronger after that talk and after being reassured once again that Suzanne is always near. I was deeply comforted, knowing she was with me in the hospital room, holding my hand as we kept watch over the man we both adored.

Another Talented Medium

Marc is a talented medium based in Florida. He is able to cross the line and speak to those who have passed on. He comes from a family of sensitives, as is so often the case with mediums. He has helped countless people heal their grief by making them understand that Spirit is near. He does this by individual sessions, by group sessions, and by phone. He has written a couple of books on Spirit as well. I can only hope my book will help those in need of healing too.

Our friend Denise had attended a group session to listen to him give a talk and thought we might like to attend one as well. Denise felt strongly he was a kind soul. He was going to make an appearance in New York City to talk to groups interested in learning what he does and perhaps to make contact with loved ones in the afterlife. Mike and I decided to go find out what he had to say and maybe be able to hear from Suzanne.

It was a hot August evening in the city when we went to listen to Marc speak. The building was in a busy section of downtown Manhattan, and when we reached the address, there was a long line waiting to get in. We were grateful that we had bought tickets online since it did not look like everyone was going to get in the door. The room was not huge, and the many people who inhabited it were all nervously hunting for chairs. All of us had lost loved ones and we all wanted to hear from them, so the tension was palatable.

After his lecture about the methods he used to reach the other side, Marc began to ask non-leading questions of the audience. After a few minutes of questions without a Spirit connection, he asked who knew "the Taurus." Well, that was Suzanne, my May baby. I yelled out, "I do! That is my daughter!"

I could feel my daughters vibration near me in the room and was certain he had connected with her. He began by telling us about her physical pain and indicating on his own body all the parts of her that had been injured and weren't functioning. Suzanne told him she had not been afraid to die. She said she was now released from all pain and discomfort. He saw or heard the band the Moody Blues, which indicated her deep depression while on Earth. He told us she was a very brave and strong Spirit (it seems that everyone acknowledged that!), who loved color and light. He described lots of lights around her now and he could see her as iridescent, wearing a flowing dress while sitting on a rock at the beach (her favorite place). The sea air was blowing her hair, and she was peaceful and angelic. Ariel, the angel of healing, came through.

He said Suzanne knew she needed to come to live with us in New York so she could die in peace with us around her. We listened to all of this with tears of emotion and joy. A small part of our own hearts began to heal with these words.

Her message to Mike that day was not to worry—she would be with him when he died (because he had been worried about that). And she wanted me to tell a good friend in San Francisco that she was always there for her. She expressed that her friends were not open to her clues that she was near, and it caused her much frustration!

The medium also said she was showing him an image of St. Joseph Aspirin and that Mike needed to take St. Joseph Aspirin every day. Such a curious statement! We did not then know that Mike had atrial fibrillation, and one of the methods of medication is a daily children's aspirin to keep the blood thin and to help prevent a stroke. After Suzanne had relayed this message for Mike, he was diagnosed and took measures to correct the problem.

Then Marc said, "I don't know why but she wants me to do this," and he suddenly performed her favorite silly funky chicken dance, which only she could do. She would move her hands up and bend her arms at the elbow, while moving in a back-and-forth fashion and dipping her knees. When she was alive, she did this dance for us all the time to be silly and make us smile.

It made everyone in the room smile and put grins on our faces. That's our girl!

All of this information made perfect sense and gave us a great deal of comfort, and a year or so later we decided to book a phone reading with Marc. Again Suzanne came through to let us know she is always around us, listening in and watching over us. Marc began to hum the songs that were stuck in my head during the day and asked me, "Does this song sound familiar? Your daughter is asking me to hum this for you. Importantly, she wants you to know she wants you to finish your book. It will be very important for others in grief to read and help heal." Among telling us other things, Suzanne indicated that she had felt like a caged bird while on Earth and now she was free and happy and busy.

Some Words of Advice

If you plan to seek out mediums, make sure their intention is one of peace and healing. Also be sure you get some references from others you trust who have spoken to the medium, and follow up. Just because people have the gift of mediumship doesn't necessarily mean they are honest or have your best interests at heart. They are human, with human failings of ego and greed. A medium or a psychic who charges an exorbitant amount of money, asks you leading questions, or asks you to buy products of any kind is one to stay away from. Also beware of those who insist you come back again for more information in exchange for more of your money. You should leave a reading feeling your session was truthful and healing.

If you have a session and your loved one does not appear, take heart. Suzanne has told us it can be hard for most Spirits to make a lot of journeys to this side, given that it can be scary and difficult to navigate the dark and uncertain places between the realms. So, it is important for you to stay open and aware, to remember there are no coincidences and Spirit communication can take many forms. It is also possible that the Spirit you wish to speak with is not ready to be contacted or to communicate just yet.

Have patience.

If you want to find the secrets of
the universe, think in
terms of energy,
frequency, and vibration.

NIKOLA TESLA, 1942

Automatic Writing

Automatic writing has been used for communication and healing for a very long time. Relaxing in front of a pen and a blank sheet of paper, or lately a computer screen and keyboard, we are able to transfer the thoughts and messages of a higher consciousness. Sitting openly and asking to hear and be heard provide insight not otherwise available to us. My daughter's words that have come to me with automatic writing or sudden intrusive thought have been enormously helpful to me in dealing with my grief and my life.

So, as I sat at my desk with pen and paper in hand, quietly thinking about Suzanne, these questions and responses filled my page. Sometimes I have asked her specific things and at other times I've just sat and waited. My questions and writing are in italic and Suzanne's messages and answers are in script and set within quotes.

I began to write to her.

What is this life all about and what do you know now?

"It is important to remember nothing is that important! We are just a chain of human existence. We need to experience being human in all of its aspects. Just BE. Love bring things into your life, and do not be afraid to throw things out that no longer work. Live all the hours and keep thinking about who this YOU is that is reflected in your existence."

During this exchange, Mike was getting ready for his second colon surgery one cold March. This was a very hard and frightening time for the two of us. It was not going to be an easy surgery and could and did have complications.

What can I do to keep calm?

"Okay, here I am. I love you, Mom—now to work. Goodness and light, laughter, and thought. God is perfection all around and in us all. Oceans of lights and love surround you. Tap into it. Believe you are the I AM. Be in the present. NOT the past. What was, was, and was meant to be. I am here with you now. Do you feel me? Yoga-meditate-exercise-dance-jump. Move your body so you are not so much in your

mind. Did you not tell me this when I was here? Now I tell you. Open to others and do not be so afraid. No one is out to hurt you. I won't let them. You have help. They are all around. Sense them—they are for you and Mike. He will be fine, but you must find other things to do. Fill your life before it is over. Help others. That's your tendency anyway—to take care of other living things.

"Move away from old things, people, and ideas. Open to the new. So much is out there to find and to see. Draw horses. They are your power animals. There is comfort in them and in their grace and good humor. Don't question—just do. We are released to do our work, each of us. I am blessed to shine in the glow. Work is reward. Our fingertips will always touch. Remember with joy, not grief."

Hard times, Suzanne. I am trying to cope. I feel lots of help, but I just can't seem to let go of the past hurts and worries. I bring them into the light circle and let go, but then later I feel them again.

"Mike's hurts are worse because you expect too much of him. He is only a man with scary things of his own. Be your own person. Don't worry about others. Worry about your space and light—how the light enfolds you—and carry that with you. Emerald green—heart chakra. His heart is heavy now-let things go.

"Wispy air—muted colors—light shining through it all. Very beautiful, and you thought flowers were amazing. The colors are soft and calm but with energy I cannot describe. Finally feeling in the right place. Not itchy anymore.

"You must dance or do yoga every day. Move, breathe in fresh air. Things you do now—think, speak, do—will have huge impressions on everyone around you. It is karma time. Send the thought forms. Review the thought-forms book [Thought-Forms by Annie Besant and C. W. Leadbeater] and think about where your head is.

"Not everyone has the gifts you do. See color, send energy. You may be compact, but your energy goes before and after you. People may be afraid of you or drawn to you because of your unusual energy. You will find your healer. Do not be surprised if it is yourself. HA! No tears, no gray, be calm."

The day of Mike's surgery arrived, and being so very unsettled and frightened, I took to my desk and wrote to her.

Will it all be okay and why am I so nervous?

"Calm down. Send healing thoughts and vibes to Mike. Your being nervous does not help. Remember how your thoughts form energy and color. Heart with wings. Green

energy. White light to surround. Be in the flow of the uni-
verse. Do not pull against it. Work with the electricity that
you are. It needs to be even and constant. Work on EVEN
AND CONSTANT. All will be well. Bring the small sketch-
book to the hospital. Forget about Mercury retrograde. It has
nothing to do with hospitals and surgery. It's in Pisces, so
more emotion and insight."

Mike's second surgery was frightening. He developed an infection during the long procedure. It went to his lungs, and he came down with double pneumonia. He was close to dying, and I lived with him in the ICU for a month where he was on a breathing machine for a week. The doctors were trying hard to figure out what bug was causing the infection. But they did save his life, and after a month in the ICU and a couple of weeks in a regular room we went home to recover. I was an emotional wreck, so I took to the computer and automatic writing in Suzanne's apartment. Looking around her place, I realized some things that I had never seen clearly before and I wrote them down.

This apartment was your space as long as you needed or
wanted it. You made it your own. You painted the walls
in the colors of the chakras: orange living room, yellow
dining room, red hallway, green entrance, violet bed-
room. Not until now did I realize what you had done.

I now know you were looking for peace and seeking to recharge your energy, trying to get your esoteric mind to recharge your spiritual energy. You had rounded the sharp corners with lights and plants and sparkly things. How do I soften the sharp edges?

"Simplify your life. Don't keep things you don't need, physically and mentally. People also, and causes. Live it simple and stress-free. We're all a little bit chipped here or there . . . small pieces out of place, the wrong fit. Nothing is perfect. I think you should strive for perfection but accept the reality that imperfection is the norm. It's more interesting, anyway. It makes us unique and who we are."

Winter with its dim light has never been my favorite time of year, for I tend to feel a heavy sadness then. I have a lot of houseplants I have had for years. Matilda, a pink begonia, is such a one.

In the following passage Suzanne chides me, saying that she is busy over there.

Matilda is looking too pale.

"Put her on the windowsill."

But I continued.

Okay, but I am not all right either. What about the healer for me?

"Try and see. Go soon. But you are yellow and stronger and clearer. I am busy here. Lots of people in pain. No answers yet. Try new things. Use crystals, rocks. See light and expand your vision. Peace."

April has always been a month of loss for me. My father, ex-husband, and our friend Brenda all passed in April. So traditionally I cringe a bit when I see April come around again. Thus, my note to Suzanne one April morning.

Suzanne, I am so weepy these last few days. I try to focus but I cannot stop going backward. How do I reset?

"Know that you are fine, and really all will be well because, as you know, all is as it should be. Distract yourself: draw, practice yoga, or knit, or read a funny book. It is the time of year that you tend to have a lock on the time/space and go back to old slots in time. You hurt this time years ago, and your mind wants to return there from habit. You must break this habit.

"There really is no time, just moments in what you call reality. Do you hear me? There are no time capsules. Time is not the same. It is not a cage. It is open and fluid. Do not be caught up in the time cage. Your body has habits of the year. Get out of them by using your mind.

"April seemed to be the bad month, but it was not. Your father was both born and released then. Brenda was released from her pain then. And Dad was also able to move out of pain then. You helped ease their pain by being in the world with them. Your father saw you as a light in his darkness—hence he felt pain because you were in pain. He did not understand that your pain was what you needed to get you HERE, to the place you are now.

"Here all is softness and light with clarity—softly luminous but clearly seen. I needed you to be my mother and I to be your daughter. Alter your sight. See beyond the obvious. Catch the energy of things and people. See the auras. Only love will make the breakthrough. THINK, relax, and let the world happen."

One afternoon I was at sixes and sevens, anxious and unable to move forward. So I asked for her help.

What can you tell me today? I feel at a loss and unsettled. I have a creative block and feel overcome by inertia.

"Life is not the end-all and be-all. It is a small part of the whole. It is hard to explain. There is transcendence through art and artists, and beauty in form and function. Must see and appreciate the breakthrough of mankind to create art and to connect with something greater and outside himself.

"The creative force moves you to another realm that is bigger, more expansive. The small self is forgotten in the bigger role. Sit and create. Knit, draw, see, make, cook. It all takes you places before unknown. I am with you then. Your mind is unlocked, open to where I am now. Wait. Know that I am always with you but when you create, I am able to be with you in a different way. Joyous, HAPPY. The heart chakra opens and is tuned. I love you, Mom."

I love you too.

And when the earth shall claim your limbs,
then shall you
truly dance.

"ON DEATH"

FROM *THE PROPHET*

BY KAHLIL GIBRAN

Dealing with Grief

After a loss, grief comes upon us like a thunderstorm, turning into a dark gray cloud surrounding us that will not easily lift into a brighter day. *Grief.* Even the word itself is forbidding. The dictionary words for grief describe the emotions that go along with the death of a loved one. Definitions of grief are put into the following descriptive words: *sorrow, misery, anguish, pain, distress, heartbreak, agony, despair.*

We have felt them all, and some of that sorrow will be with us forever. However, our lives can be made easier by knowing Spirit is not far away.

How many times have you heard that you should just get on with your life? Or just get over it? That you should stop talking about your loved one and that you would be better off if you did not speak of your memories? Well, I believe you should not take any of that advice. I believe you should keep your loved one with you—alive in your heart and your mind. After all, they are not so far away. The energy is constant and unwavering, and you should take peace in this knowledge. Look for your postcards and your messages. Take comfort in the nearness of Spirit. We cannot hug our loved ones as we once did but we can acknowledge their presence.

Learned people have said grief is a process, not an event. We need to remember this process is long, maybe lifelong. I would like to share some of the techniques I found useful when in the depths of grief. I believe I am still in some grief after having lost my daughter and in many ways always will be, but we share so much joy now. I know she is happy, and with me when I need her. I know I need to live my life with an open heart. Though I am not completely healed, I am comforted.

The point of dealing with grief is to get us to a calm and open place so we can hear and see Spirit when contact is made and move forward with our lives—make peace with ourselves. A person clothed in the grayness of grief cannot be reached by Spirit, however hard they might try. A calm mind and an open heart allow those postcards from loved ones to be discovered.

I have found that grief has many sides, including depression, anxiety, guilt, and anger. While grieving, at times we feel so very depressed, it's as if another moment cannot be endured. It is too much to stand, to eat, to breathe. At other times we are so full of anxiety and the thoughts of "what if" and "why" that we can't focus, we cannot be present for anyone, and sleep just will not happen. After some therapy, at times I found myself very angry at Suzanne for leaving me. I had planned for her to be with us until the end of our lives, not hers. I was also angry with myself for not being able to save her. I am her mother, after all. That was my job, wasn't it? I needed to reconcile all of these emotions in a place of peace and forgiveness.

Grief will sometimes catch you unawares, no matter how much time has passed since your loved one has passed on. Something will trigger a memory or a feeling, and then we are hit with it in the sensitive scar tissue around the heart. You may feel if you breathe or move a single muscle or think another thought, you will certainly collapse into a small heap, unable to bear another moment of consciousness.

In the beginning I found that, to be able to cope in those moments, it was necessary to withdraw into a dark and silent self-made cave for a short while in order to once again face life and reality. But we are here, and we must bravely face the rest of our life and, as Suzanne has said, "to evolve."

This means, of course, that we have to be ready to talk about our loss to those who are unaware of our pain. When you meet new people, the conversation will inevitably turn to talk of children, spouses, grandchildren, and questions about them. This can be extremely hard. Some people cope by not even mentioning the lost loved one but I'm not sure this is healthy for healing, nor does it honor the life lived.

A woman I met on a trip soon after Suzanne had passed asked me how many children I had. I responded by saying, "I have two daughters and one just recently died." This was the first time I had to answer that question and I wasn't ready for it. Of course, tears rolled down my face—they were unable to be stopped. The woman looked stricken and said, "I am so sorry I asked you." But I answered, "No, it's okay. You need to be able to ask and I need to be able to answer with love and not tears," as I do now. This takes a bit of practice and some time. We need to be able to answer questions about our loss with equanimity, with joy in their lives, and to express our love with grace.

Now, when I am caught in a difficult memory of pain and suffering, I catch myself and feel Suzanne's presence admonishing me to stop and remember she is always with me in some form and that she will be there every step of my life. Her Spirit is so joyful and happy, it can turn my mood into thankfulness that she is in a good place and has successfully completed her time on Earth. So must we all.

Beware, however, that grief can become almost a strange place of comfort. In that place you may feel you can still hold the persons Spirit close and shut out the world. This is not fair to others who loved that person and not fair to yourself. However, there is a healthier way to be with Spirit. You can begin to transform the awful darkness into light for you and for those around you.

Death is a move to the light—to the next plane of existence. If you can focus on the happiness and end of suffering for your loved one and be thankful for your Earthly time together, your life can be worth living again. All those postcards surely help.

The Stress of Loss

Loss is extremely stressful, and you need to do everything in your power to find acceptance about what's happened and how your life is now altered. The medical profession has agreed that broken heart syndrome is real. Intense grief can cause a sudden death in someone extremely close to the deceased, as happened with my grandmother and her favorite son, and with Debbie Reynolds and her daughter, Carrie Fisher.

The loss can be just too great for the heart to handle. Intense grief can cause the heart to beat in an irregular way, leading to cardiac stress, which can lead to death. We know that for some people under the extreme emotion of grief, the heart can even change shape, thereby weakening the left ventricle and causing cardiac distress or a heart attack. Dying of a broken heart was noted in a study in *Psychology Today* in 2012 by the American Heart Association, as reported in the *AARP News Bulletin* in January/February 2019 and *The New York Times* on March 24, 2019.

We must be very careful with our grief. Here are some of the things I have learned about dealing with grief. I hope these suggestions can help you too.

Make Changes Slowly

I suggest you do not be in a hurry to make changes. Sit with things for a while. Please do not give into the pressure of others who think ridding yourself of possessions that belonged to the loved one will make you feel better, or "because it is time." You alone will know when it is time. It may never be time.

Good-hearted friends tried to help me when Suzanne died by clearing out some things in her cluttered apartment so guests for the memorial would be more comfortable staying there. I miss those things. I think about them and wish I had been able to have the time to properly sort through the memories they contained instead of removing them in a rush in order to make others feel better. In retrospect, it would have been much better to do things that made *me* feel better instead. In good time I might have let those things go with a happy countenance, but not when I was grieving and confused.

Accept the Endgame

We know someone who was at his longtime friend's side when he passed into Spirit. He held his hand and was present through all of his suffering. Now he is troubled by the fact that when he thinks of his buddy, all he can remember is the difficult "endgame" and not the good times. The end of his friend's life, and not the many good and happy times he shared with him, is where his mind wishes to return.

Our brains and our hearts do this to us since our loss is so great and traumatic. I am not a health care professional by any means, and I am not sure why we do this, but I assured him that over time those memories of pain and suffering would fade a bit. Perhaps it is the way our minds keep us connected or perhaps we then beat ourselves up for any guilt we may feel over the relationship—all of the "should have ... why didn't I?" questions that we now cannot easily answer.

We can help the healing process by consciously releasing the thoughts of suffering when they happen and replacing them with memories of good times full of love and laughter. We celebrate the life lived and remember the loving marks this Spirit made on us. As Suzanne has often said, "Celebrate my life—my death was such a small part of me." Spirit does not want us to remember the endgame. I cannot say this enough, and I repeat it to myself in those dark times when the endgame catches me unawares.

Yoga

Yoga has been second nature for me for most of my life. I taught hatha yoga in Los Angeles for many years after learning it in Hollywood in the late 1960s. Some days I had six full classes of asana and meditation. I still begin every day with an hour of yoga, but I found I had to discipline myself to continue in the darkest days. However, once I again begin to move through the breathing and the physical postures, I find my mind and body start to loosen up, calm down, and refresh itself.

If yoga is new to you, I suggest you learn it first from an accomplished teacher in a private setting. Your closely held emotions can be set loose by the movements and the breathing, and you should be able to confront your feelings in a healing place. An open class may not be best in the beginning.

There are many types of yoga, and in each style every teacher will have a different method. While some styles and teachers are calming, others focus more on the physical aspect and are more athletic in nature. Hatha yoga combines poses, breath work, and often some meditation, while Ashtanga yoga is a vigorous workout. Kundalini yoga is all about breath work, and I think is a useful style to practice in times of grief.

Ask if you can take a trial class before you sign up for several weeks to make sure the style and the teacher resonate with you and your needs.

Breath Work

Breath work is most important for you during this time. When we are stressed, we tend to hold our breath or to breathe shallowly. You need lots of good oxygen now to help your mind and body recover and be healthy. Proper deep breathing is a good way to begin to calm your mind and relax your body when you're anxious, or to create energy when you're depressed and you find yourself down that rabbit hole, unable to get out. Try these simple breathing routines to create either peace or energy within yourself.

To obtain the most benefit from your breath during these routines, use diaphragmatic breathing, or what some call stomach or belly breathing. Just be sure to breathe through your nose and not your mouth.

- *Place your hand gently on your abdomen. This will help you feel your belly move outward in an inhale and inward on the exhale.*

- *As you inhale, push your stomach outward against your hand to allow the lungs to completely fill.*

- *As you exhale, draw the belly in to help expel the breath. Feel your hand move inward, following your belly.*

There are many breathing techniques, but the following two simple, counted breaths are very easy to do and are very effective. Do at least four or five repetitions at a time. You can do them anywhere and anytime you feel anxious or exhausted. Sit, stand, or lie down flat, in a comfortable position, and clear your mind of other thought. Try to concentrate only on the evenness of the breath.

- *To create a sense of calmness or peace:*
  Inhale gently to the count of four and exhale deeply to the count of eight.
  Repeat this several times and relax. You might think it impossible to exhale twice as much as you inhale but you will be surprised. We are conditioned to take a deep in-breath, not a deep out-breath. Try it. It is an effective method to relax at night when sleep just will not come, or anytime you feel panic or anxiety setting in.

- *To create some energy:*
  Inhale gently to the count of four and exhale gently to the count of four.
  Repeat this several times and relax for a few minutes. Then repeat several times again. This is best to do in the morning or the afternoon when your energy is low, or you feel depression coming on.

Meditation

Often in the midst of grief and loss, our minds lose focus and we can't seem to accomplish much. We are irritated, grumpy, and sad all at the same time. Our normal diversions like film, books, computer games, and social media are not helpful. Try some meditation. Meditation helps the mind rest and renews you and provides some peace. A simple practice of even five minutes is so helpful, even though it might seem impossible at first. Please give it a chance.

Sit in a quiet place, with your spine straight and your feet flat on the floor. You can keep your eyes open and unfocused or close them gently. You can support your back against the back of the chair. Just concentrate on the breath as it flows in and flows out. There is no need to count your breaths, just breathe. Try to let go of the many thoughts that will continue to march through by just gently dismissing them and returning to the breath.

Make no judgment on the intrusive thoughts. Our brains never rest, so these crazy thoughts are normal. Dismissing them and going back to your breath is your goal. In the beginning, try to do this for just five minutes. You can slowly increase the time by five-minute stretches to thirty minutes or more, but do not push yourself. You need not do more than this beginning process to feel you have given your mind a rest.

There are many classes on mindfulness and meditation. You can explore the different methods and choose the one that is right for you. There are online meditations to download to a device, and many books to learn from. Also, classes and meditation groups that provide some important community are readily available.

Practice Your Faith

It goes without saying that, whatever your faith, the teachings you believe in will get you through the darkest days. It seems that all religions have rituals regarding death that provide some succor for the bereaved. We need our rituals and beliefs after a death to put some grounding back into our lives. There is much community in religious groups. Being with people can be painful at first, but really is good for your mental state. We are social animals and we need each other.

I am thankful every day that the rector of our church was there for me when I needed wise counsel.

Join a Support Group

Being with others who have recently traveled your path gives comfort and allows you to understand the grief of others, as well as understand that you are not alone in your experience. Many churches and community centers offer a specific grief group for very little or no cost.

We need to tell the story of our loved one and relay what our loss has meant. Family and friends become exhausted by this long before we do. I need to talk about Suzanne even if it makes others uncomfortable. I talked about my daughter when she was alive, and I still must talk about her now. Her importance in my life did not stop because she is not physically here for those people to see. I have two daughters and they are both important to me. Support groups and therapists seem to have unending patience and compassion—far more, I have found, than do family and friends.

Hiding bad moments to make others in our lives feel better is not healthy. All of that suppressed sadness and angst will not only make us ill but can destroy relationships. Support groups and therapists are there to let you talk and to heal in your own time.

One-on-One Therapy

Therapy was very helpful to me after Suzanne died. It allowed me to unburden myself in a safe place without any sort of judgments or reciprocal emotions. If affordable, talking to a qualified therapist one-on-one allows your feelings to flood and be dealt with in a way that friends and family just cannot provide. It is unfortunate that therapy is often not covered by our medical insurance system when, in times of great loss, the benefits are so evident. I deeply hope that will change.

Be sure to choose a therapist who deals with grief as well as well-being. These people are trained to help, and you will find great solace in talking to them. All therapists will not be open to Spirit, but it seems that all of them will understand the sense of great loss and can help you with the inevitable feelings of anger and perhaps guilt as well.

Dealing with Anger

If you are angry, processing your anger in a nondestructive way is one of the hardest things to do. For one thing, it is hard to acknowledge you are even angry with loved ones who have passed over. Those loved ones have probably been through suffering and pain before transitioning and it just doesn't feel right to be angry with them. But no doubt you are angry. Angry that they left you, that they caused you suffering too, and that perhaps they didn't tie up the loose ends as you and the family would have liked. There are so many other personal reasons unique to your relationship that can cause you to be angry with them after they've died.

I remember one evening walking home from group therapy at dusk. We had discussed anger during the session, and I expressed the fact that I really did not feel any anger at all. I just felt the usual sadness, depression, and frustration of loss. Then I noticed a figure ahead of me. The person was walking a small dog on one of those

I Am Here

elastic leashes. I determined that it was a woman and she was walking very slowly; the dog crisscrossed the entire sidewalk as it wandered.

I was in the normal New York hurry. All of a sudden, I felt tremendous rage at this woman and her dog. My body stiffened, the pressure rose in my throat, and I clenched my jaw. I thought to myself that if that woman did not move aside, I would kick her dog as far as I could and then go after *her*. Now, I am a peaceful person and I love all animals. Never would I hurt a sentient being, but I was going after that dog and that woman! I luckily came to my senses and realized what this anger was about. It was not about the woman and her dog but really about Suzanne for leaving and anger at myself for not being able to do anything about it.

Unexpressed anger can make you sick. It can also prevent a Spirit from contacting you due to the negative energy that unexpressed anger produces. How can you release it without causing yourself or others harm? I found the obvious yelling, screaming, and smashing of things (in a careful way) really did help. Any extra crockery around that you have been meaning to get rid of? Writing down my anger in a letter and then tearing it up got my feelings on paper and let me actually see what I was angry about. Abusing pillows was a favorite: throwing them, punching them, screaming into them, and squishing them let my feelings run their course.

135

Hard physical work has always been a productive way to diffuse anger. My kitchen floors never looked so good and my garden was without a weed while my anger was boiling over. Chop wood, build a fence, or otherwise exhaust yourself until your conscious self is calm again.

Guilt

Try not to load guilt on to your grief. Why didn't I do more? Maybe I could have done more . . . something to prevent this death of my child, spouse, friend, parent. Guilt is a hard cross to bear. *If only I had . . .* comes to mind and preys on your thoughts of the day and the dreams of the night. Doing this to yourself about an event that cannot be changed will only damage you, both mentally and physically. I have no perfect remedy except to suggest you seek outside help so you can see clearly. Therapists, healers, spiritual counselors, and mediums can provide you with tools to deal with feelings of guilt. Your loved one does not want you to suffer these feelings. Many of the events of our lives play out just as they should, based on decisions we've made in this life and other lifetimes. Forgive yourself for any perceived mistakes and go forward to the present moment. As Suzanne has said, "Leave the past behind."

Go forward into the rest of your life.

Physical Care

I was never so sick with colds and flu as during the first year of Suzanne's passing. I could not seem to get well. The body mourns in many ways.

Since the mind and body are deeply connected, for sure a cold or the flu will happen. Your immune system will be overstressed. Therefore, you must tend to your body in the most caring way possible. Although appetite is often gone during the first stages of grief, you still must nourish yourself. Easily digestible soups, smoothies, gentle vegetables and fruits are more important now than ever. Our gut is our second brain. Emotional tumult leads to digestive upset, stomach pain, and weight loss. Think about relaxing your stomach muscles when you eat, and stop and breathe before swallowing. Life is hard to swallow sometimes. Be kind to yourself.

Short-term answers like alcohol and drugs may help for a bit, but when they wear off, you are still you trying to deal with a life-altering event that cannot be changed. Coming through this in a healthy way may be the hardest thing you will ever do. Put your body in the strongest position possible so you can open yourself up to Spirit, find those postcards, smile again, and go on with your life.

Places and Tools of Renewal

Each of us has places we travel to in time of stress. Find yours and try to go there, even if only in your thoughts.

For some of us it is a sandy beach by the water. For others it's a forest or a park, or even our own personal garden or quiet room.

For me a walk in the forested area of New York's Central Park is heavenly. Hearing and seeing the birds and observing the seasonal changes in the plants and flowers give me a sense of peace and wonder. I see God in nature and feel very connected to the cycle of life while feeling the presence of Spirit. I am comforted by the fact that energy in nature is constantly transformed but never lost. The journey never ends but merely changes form.

I am also blessed to have a balcony here in New York City that serves as my garden of renewal. I fill it with flowering plants and herbs, and it gives me things to care for. A garden needs tending. When your loved one no longer needs tending, it leaves a big absence in your life. The absence can be filled by tending to other growing things that need you now. Even a simple houseplant can help. When a plant dies, it is also a reminder that no one or nothing is eternal. We are all here temporarily—part of the continuous movement of life and death.

A wise woman told me to perform an "act of beauty" to change my energy from negative to positive. This could take many forms: create something, bring home flowers, paint a wall a favorite color. But doing a kindness for a being who is suffering is a perfect act of beauty. While helping another, we help ourselves.

A Date Is Just a Date

I found I needed to stop mourning the anniversaries of Suzanne's birth and her death. Instead, I needed to celebrate them. I needed to celebrate the fact that I was given the gift of her life with me and also that she was released from this hard school of learning. I suggest circling those important calendar dates in bright colors, prepare celebratory food, and raise a toast to an amazing life. These are not days to grieve but to be happy for a life lived for as long as it was granted—a life where much was learned, however long or short the time here. One day, quicker than we realize, we will all be together again in fullness. Of course we miss our loved ones terribly, and our hearts will always contain holes because of their physical absence, but try to leave those thoughts behind and celebrate the fact of their release from here to there.

Pets

Should you be so lucky as to have a pet, now is the time to let the pet's innate healing power work on you. Dogs and cats feel our moods and want our vibrations to be without pain. Often a cat has curled up by me when I have been ill or sad, and it's not left my side until I felt better. Dogs know us very well too, and are happy when we are happy. Doctors and therapists now acknowledge the importance of animals for our psyche and recommend them for emotional health. Rescue animals are most grateful for a new home. Why not help each other out? It is awfully difficult to completely give into grief when the cat demands food or an ear rub or the dog nudges you for a walk outside where you must breathe in the fresh air.

Compassion

Sometimes I would forget that my husband, Mike, and my daughter, Jennifer, were grieving too. Everyone who loved Suzanne went through grief of their own. We tend to believe that our suffering is far worse than that of others. To you it certainly is, but your loss has not happened in a vacuum. Others who loved that person are also in pain. Family members mourn, friends mourn, even pets mourn. Pain of loss is universal, and, like a spider's web, when the web is touched, the pain radiates outward to all within it. Be gentle with others who grieve with you. When behaving in compassionate ways to others, it may lessen the pain in the world around us.

Moments of Mortality

When we lose someone, we stare death in the face. We come up close to our own mortality. We too will die one day. Others we care about will die also. For most of us, this is unnerving, scary, and can seem very dark. If we can come to grips with the idea of impermanence and change, that nothing here is immortal or static, then we can begin to relax and accept loss, and the change in our lives that a death brings.

Spirit has reassured us of the afterlife. Suzanne has reassured me of her happiness, joy and the fact of her presence when I need her. There is nothing to fear of death, and knowing this, we find our grief from the loss of loved ones here on Earth is eased.

When Is It Finished?

There will be long stretches of time when you feel calm, happy, and full of acceptance of the loss. The memories triggered by the sense of that Spirit's presence or a post-card found will give you a smile and an inner joy. *Ah*, you think, *I have passed the stages of inconsolable grief.* Maybe not. I find that grief still catches me unawares with a pain so sharp I must try to catch my breath—to take a moment away until I can come back to life as it is now. I still howl and fall for a bit into the abyss, but I can climb out, knowing that Suzanne is holding my hand on the way up.

This is not a failure—it is the reality of loss here on Earth. It is okay to have those moments, but it's not okay to dwell on them. I hear Suzanne saying when I slip into grief, "Don't go there, Mom. I am happy, and I want you to be happy too. Remember, I am here." We must live for the living while keeping the dead close.

I came across the following paragraph on a friend's Facebook page and I found it beautiful, timely, and something to think about. It is a quote he posted from Henry Scott Holland

"Death is nothing at all. It does not count. I have only slipped away into the next room. Nothing has happened. Everything remains exactly as it was. I am I, and you are you, and the old life that we lived so fondly together is untouched, unchanged. Whatever we were to each other, that we are still. Call me by the old familiar name. Speak of me in the easy way which you always used. Put no difference into your tone. Wear no forced air of solemnity or sorrow. Laugh as we always laughed at the little jokes that we enjoyed together. Play, smile, think of me, pray for me. Let my name be ever the household word that it always was. Let it be spoken without an effort, without the ghost of a shadow upon it, life means all that it ever meant. It is the same as it ever was. There is absolute and unbroken continuity. What is this death but a negligible accident? Why should I be out of mind because I am out of sight? I am but waiting for you, for an interval, somewhere very near, just around the corner. All is well." Death is Nothing at All *by Henry Scott Holland.*

"I Am Here."

Acknowledgments

My deep gratitude to everyone who made this book possible. Special thanks to Vassim Abdullah, who, as my first reader, gave me much appreciated encouragement to tell my story. My daughter, Jennifer, was always ready to give me needed support, although I know full well that she had grief of her own. Many thanks to Linda Gundel, Nancy Genser, Chris Santini, Denise Craig, Daria Lambone, and Donna Hennen for always being there. And thank you to my friend Jeff Peters for his special insight.

There are no words to express my love and gratitude to my husband, Michael. He read and re-read my writing and therefore relived every experience multiple times. He is my rock.

I have such appreciation for Dan Alexandar at New York Book Editors for finding me the wonderful people who actually made my words a book: Susan Olinsky

for the amazing cover art, Anne Dillon for the excel-
lent copy edit, and the kind and knowledgeable Tim
McConnehey and his team at Izzard Ink.

About the Author

Judith Jones Togher grew up in Los Angeles, attended the University of California at Long Beach, married and raised two daughters. As a young woman, she learned Hatha Yoga at the Sivananda Center and received a teaching certificate at Clara Spring Studios in Hollywood. She taught Hatha Yoga and meditation for over twenty years. After being widowed, she also wrote documentation for large corporations while continuing to run her yoga business.

After her children were grown, she moved to New York City to write product documentation and to help market products to international banks, while keeping her hand in yoga, meditation and the study of Buddhism and metaphysics.

She met her husband, Michael, in New York and they remain happily retired in Manhattan.

www.ingramcontent.com/pod-product-compliance
Lightning Source LLC
La Vergne TN
LVHW011234080426
835509LV00005B/501